MW00721558

IVANHOE

The Mask of Chivalry

TWAYNE'S MASTERWORK STUDIES

Robert Lecker, General Editor

IVANHOE

The Mask of Chivalry

Paul J. deGategno

TWAYNE PUBLISHERS • NEW YORK
Maxwell Macmillan Canada • Toronto
Maxwell Macmillan International • New York Oxford Singapore Sydney

Twayne's Masterwork Studies No. 125

Twayne Publishers   Maxwell Macmillan Canada, Inc.
Macmillan Publishing Company   1200 Eglinton Avenue East
866 Third Avenue   Suite 200
New York, New York 10022   Don Mills, Ontario M3C 3N1

Library of Congress Cataloging-in-Publication Data
DeGategno, Paul J.
    Ivanhoe : the mask of chivalry / Paul J. deGategno.
        p.   cm.—(Twayne's masterworks studies; MWS 125)
    Includes bibliographical references and index.
    ISBN 0-8057-9438-7 (hard)—ISBN 0-8057-8379-2 (pbk.)
    1. Scott, Walter, Sir, 1771–1832. Ivanhoe. 2. Great Britain—History—Richard I,
1189{en}1199—Historiography. 3. Knights and knighthood in literature. 4. Chivalry
in literature. I. Title. II. Series.
PR5318.D43 1994
823'.914—dc20   93-29454
                                                                           CIP

The paper used in this publication meets the minimum requirements of American
National Standard for Information Sciences—Permanence of Paper for Printed
Library Materials, ANSI Z39.48-1984.∞ ™

10 9 8 7 6 5 4 3 2 1

Printed in the United States of America.

To Veronica and Paul deGategno

Contents

Note on the References and Acknowledgments

All references to *Ivanhoe* are to the 1986 Penguin edition, edited with an introduction by A. N. Wilson, which is based on the 1830 Opus Magnum edition and incorporates Walter Scott's revisions.

I have been teaching Walter Scott and *Ivanhoe* for a number of years and am grateful to all the students who have studied his work with me, and most especially to the students in my Literature Honors course at Wesleyan College, who heard an early version of this book in the form of lectures.

I wish to thank Wayne Martin, who did an excellent job as my research assistant during his internship; my colleagues in the English department, especially Linda Flowers, Leverett Smith, Steve Ferebee, Vivienne Anderson, and Christopher LaLonde; and my friends at Bragg, Terry Moore, Brian Williams, and Mike Mullins, who have listened to me and read much of this study. Thanks also to the staff of the Pearsall Library, Wesleyan College, especially the invaluable Dianne Taylor. Particular thanks to Linda Skojec for thorough, diligent typing of the manuscript.

I am happy to acknowledge the generous support of the Wesleyan College Faculty Research Committee for a grant, and the Board of Trustees of the College for giving me a semester sabbatical to start the book. I am grateful to Robert Lecker, the general editor, for his intelligent advice and for the chance to contribute this volume to the series.

My wife and children have borne with me and this book beyond the call of duty, and for that I remain in their debt.

To my parents, who will understand the nature of my gratitude, I dedicate this book.

Sir Walter Scott
Portrait by Sir Henry Raeburn, 1822. Courtesy of The Scottish National
Portrait Gallery.

Chronology: Sir Walter Scott's Life and Works

1771	Walter Scott born 15 August in the College Wynd, Edinburgh, the ninth child of Walter Scott, Writer to the Signet, and Anne Rutherford.
1773	Contracts infantile paralysis (polio), which leaves him permanently lame. Sent to his grandfather Robert Scott's farm at Sandyknowe in the Borders.
1775	Robert Scott dies and Walter Scott returns to Edinburgh to live in father's new house in George Square. Travels to England.
1775	American Revolution.
1776	Adam Smith, *Wealth of Nations*.
1779	In October, enters the High School in Edinburgh as a second year student.
1783	Graduates from the High School, having spent his leisure hours prodding a vivid and active imagination by reading on all subjects. In September, England acknowledges American independence at the Peace of Paris. In November, enrolls at Edinburgh College in Latin, Greek, and logic classes.
1785	First large clearances of Highland families.
1786	In March, begins five-year apprenticeship at his father's law office.
1786–1787	Meets Robert Burns, who had just published *Poems Chiefly in the Scottish Dialect*.
1789–1791	Studies civil and Scots law at Edinburgh University. French Revolution begins.
1791	Admitted to Speculative Society, a debating club of young advocates.

1819	Publishes *The Bride of Lammermoor* and *A Legend of Montrose,* as *Tales of My Landlord, Third Series.* Begins dictating *Ivanhoe* in May, published in three volumes 18 December (often dated 1820); 10,000 copies sold in a month.
1820	Death of George III; accession of George IV. Publication of *The Monastery* and *The Abbot.* Elected president of the Royal Society, Edinburgh. Tendered honorary degrees from Oxford and Cambridge. At least seven versions of *Ivanhoe* produced for the stage in 1820.
1821	Publication of *Kenilworth* and *The Pirate.*
1822	Publication of *The Fortunes of Nigel.* Serves as master of ceremonies for the visit of George IV to Scotland in August.
1823	Publication of *Peveril of the Peak, Quentin Durward,* and *St. Ronan's Will.* Chosen by The Royal Academy, London, as professor of ancient history.
1824	*Redgauntlet.*
1825	*Tales of the Crusaders (The Betrothed, The Talisman).* Begins journal in November.
1826	Following the financial crash of 1825, Scott finds himself and his partner, James Ballantyne, involved in the ruin of their publishing house, Ballantyne and Constable. His personal liability: £130,000. Wife dies. In Paris, sees a Rossini opera of *Ivanhoe.* Publication of *Woodstock.*
1827	Publishes *Chronicles of the Canongate,* a series of short stories, and the first volume of *The Life of Napoleon Buonaparte.*
1828	Publication of *The Fair Maid of Perth.* Prepares *Opus Magnum,* a complete annotated edition of his works.
1829	Publication of *Anne of Geierstein* and *Tales of My Landlord, Fourth Series (Count Robert of Paris).*
1830	Death of George IV and accession of William IV.
1831	Suffers from first stroke, which results in apoplectic paralysis. Cruises the Mediterranean in a naval vessel put at his disposal.
1832	Publishes *Castle Dangerous.* Dies 21 September at Abbotsford and is buried beside his wife at Dryburgh Abbey.

LITERARY AND HISTORICAL
CONTEXT

1

Cultural Contexts and Sir Walter Scott

Nearly two centuries ago Sir Walter Scott was considered the greatest of all British novelists, a writer whose genius compared favorably with Shakespeare's.

A Scotsman, he was born during one of the most progressive periods in his country's history. The progress of the Scottish Enlightenment had brought rapid change, permitting a freedom of spirit both of mind and body. Scottish agriculture between 1760 and 1820 improved, more modern methods reducing somewhat the effects of periodic famines, at least in the lowlands. Industry and commerce, though not as great as in England, were being transformed by the revolution in production, methods of transport, the organization of trade, and the widening of credit. There was growth in all areas of economic and social life.

Highland life, as it had been known before the last Jacobite defeat in 1745, was gone, especially its traditional political jurisdictions. The tribal system, with its patriarchal clan chief, had lost its hold on the people. The forced leveling of the Highland way of life did bring, however, for all of its insensitivity and cruelty, a uniformity with the rest of Scotland. Law, land tenure, education, and religion became similar institutions for both Highlander and Lowlander alike.

For all our contemporary interest in Highland culture, we must acknowledge Scott as a product of Edinburgh, the cultural capital of Scotland. With the rise of the Scottish Enlightenment, Edinburgh became preeminent as a center of intellectual activity. During its high period in the late eighteenth century its university, sophisticated literati, and increasing political importance fostered the continued growth of a social elite. Despite the Act of Union in 1707, which has often been cited as depleting Scotland of its best citizens, it is more accurate to say that lesser nobility and gentry did not leave Edinburgh in large numbers. London may have had a small resident Scottish community; Edinburgh, however, remained the home of the majority of Scots of rank and property. Not until the end of the eighteenth century does one find this group seriously breaking apart, its traditional base taken over by a new bourgeois professional society.

As a poet and novelist, Walter Scott chose to explain the nature of the task facing the Scottish nation as it grappled with a new future. His method depended on what many have called a new historical outlook, historicism, particularly its chief characteristic, the doctrine of organic unity. Scott's novels employ a view supporting the unity of historical phenomena in an evolutionary pattern of growth. Whether one is reading *Waverley* or *Ivanhoe,* often seen as quite different works, the past seems deeply attuned to the nation's conception of itself, as well as directly tied to its present fortunes, an organically intertwined system of institutions and values.[1]

What prompts his novels into action are conflicts both universal and real; though the focus may fall on a precise time, the motivations of characters seem unconstrained by such precision. Scott's complex attitudes toward his own life and the lives of his characters reflect the processes of social change going on during the Napoleonic wars and the postwar period. The impulse for conserving the past and the instinct for progress—a present that would liberate humanity from the weight of past failures—complete a portrait of the artist. Scottish common-sense philosophy, his own pragmatic restatement of eighteenth-century Enlightenment thought, and current social reforms in England

4

and Scotland all encouraged Scott's acceptance of the law of the necessary progress of society through successive stages. One might argue for *Ivanhoe* as happy evidence of his coming to terms with this process.

Complicating this process, and surely adding to Scott's vision as he surveyed the scene, was the transition in Europe from war to peace. The defeat of Napoleon in 1815 had given England tremendous power abroad: not only among its European neighbors—with whom it had wielded significant influence at the Congress of Vienna while deciding on how best to restrain France from future aggression—but also with its new colonial gains. In the Indian Ocean, the Caribbean, the Mediterranean, and the Aegean and in the critical sea passage at the Cape of Good Hope, England now became the supreme imperial power in the world. Supremacy in trade and commerce would be undisputed for nearly a century. At home the English constitution had served the people and the country well during the war—and generally industrialists and merchants had prospered. The growth of factories and the sale of manufactured goods seemed to ensure England's economic health in this new world order.

Unfortunately, this accelerated change was being ushered in with a righteous call for traditional conservatism. In Europe various monarchies resorted to their traditional claims to legitimacy, now that the Napoleonic threat was over, and the Catholic Church resumed its influence, as did its worst aberration, the Spanish Inquisition. In England the public soon turned its attention away from its national heroes, Wellington and Castlereagh, and focused instead on the country's growing unemployment problems and the simmering antagonisms of its class system.

England had existed for considerable time with deep divisions in its society. The nobility and gentry continued their monopoly of political life, the great landed estates, their church, and their pocket boroughs. The middle classes had grown significantly in size and diversity by the early nineteenth century, but for all their increased wealth they were largely excluded from political power. Finally, the great mass of the poor—mostly depressed agricultural workers living from one harvest to another, with no hope of competing successfully with the established landowners or the uneducated and brutalized industrial laborer, often exploited and threatened with sudden unemployment—were living in the most desperate circumstances.

The law and the church—the usual champions of the poor—were inadequate to the complications of a rising population, the creation of new industrial towns, and the effects of the French and American revolutions. The traditional institutions had not reformed their standard of conduct with regard to the less privileged. Parliament had not shifted its focus from ministering to the King to servicing the needs of the people. Without reform in a broad sense, no real progress could be made in correcting the ills of society.

Yet the horrors and excesses of the French Revolution had frightened the landed aristocracy from proposing any changes. Reform proposals were viewed as radical, and the atmosphere between rich and poor remained strained. Any demonstration by the poor—the mobs—caused unreasoned fear in the rest of society. Even the most legitimate discontent was viewed as a prelude to open insurrection. The forces of industrial development and rapid urbanization were further aggravated with the demobilization of 400,000 soldiers and the end of huge government contracts—both meant economic upheaval.

Lord Liverpool's administration (1812–27) remained unimaginative and repressive. The government sought only to protect vested interests in agriculture and industry, while accusing the people of plotting to overthrow Parliament. The passage of the Corn Law of 1815 excluded foreign grain and protected the price of native wheat. It accomplished little except to anger the poor, who were forced to buy costly bread. Agitators demanding reform in great meetings, one held at Spa Fields, London, in 1816, brought only the repressive Coercion Acts of 1817, suspending habeas corpus and increasing penalties for seditious assembly. The lower classes had already taken out their anger on industry in the Luddite riots (1811–16) by smashing new machinery, blaming it for their poverty. But with the loss of food, as well as their jobs, the poor again clamored for change.

A meeting in August 1819 in St. Peter's Field, Manchester, ended in calamity. Sixty thousand people had marched carrying banners proclaiming "Universal Suffrage" and "Reform Now" to hear a well-known radical orator. Immediately, the authorities became intimidated, attempted to arrest the speaker, and finally felt the necessity of using troops to disperse the crowd, with some casualties. But the tension between rich and poor had reached a climax here in what was ironically renamed the Peterloo Massacre. The government retaliated with the Six Acts in December to curb public agitation and the press. Some of these measures were reasonable, but at the time the public felt the government had shown once again its reactionary character. Feelings rose to such heights that extremists plotted to blow up the entire cabinet at dinner and seize the Bank of England. This so-called Cato Street Conspiracy raised for a time the government's prestige and further set back reform agitation.

While many writers, Lord Byron, Robert Southey, and William Hazlitt among them, maintained political relationships with their readers, Scott avoided controversy and single-minded attacks on the government. He pursued reform without advocating civil war, warned of the changes involved in past reconciliations between opposing parties, and generally pressed for complex solutions to difficult problems. No idealizing of the past would do, in Scott's mind; change would bring an uneasy peace where strong leadership would be required to achieve a just and stable society.

2

Literary Contexts

Why do we continue to read *Ivanhoe?* The question would have been laughable in the short period after its publication in late 1819, when the entire first printing of 10,000 copies was sold in two weeks and six dramatic productions based on the book were performed within a year. Aside from the heat of that moment, readers today have continued their love affair with *Ivanhoe* for three reasons.

For one thing, there is the color and romantic vision of the medieval age. Scott invokes the twelfth century with all the flair and enjoyment embodied in the curiosity of the late eighteenth and early nineteenth centuries for that remote time. What gives *Ivanhoe* its charm, of course, is that Scott unashamedly writes of knights, kings, and distressed ladies acting under the impulse of love, religious faith, or a mere desire for adventure. At the same moment he represents the plight of individuals whose lives are caught up in the collapse of feudalism.

A second source of Scott's lasting appeal lies in his exploiting his own classic formula for the historical novel. Ironically, critics have complained of the novel's lack of historical accuracy, but *Ivanhoe* succeeds because it is a brilliant piece of myth making. Characters—over 150 of them—do not display complex psychological impulses; instead, they embrace their fates as determined in the variety and contradictions of the historical moment. Scott's historic conception of the evolution of society—its class struggles—shapes them. They, however, represent the mood of the generation of nineteenth-century readers who found themselves closely connected to the political events then disturbing the social calm. Whether Scott's character leads the assault on a medieval fortress or stands apart observing from the vastness of the forest, he must weigh the shifting forces of the cultural conflict, one age dying and the other struggling to emerge. Scott encourages moral freedom in his characters—each is free to choose for good or ill. For all *Ivanhoe's* sensitivity to the past, the consciousness of its characters remains an intrinsically modern response, not a medieval one. The important role of the Catholic church in twelfth-century England remains unexamined, and Scott's depiction of the Normans and Saxons at each other's throats 130 years after the Conquest cannot be supported by the historical evidence. But readers have continued to accept with fascination the illusion and admire "the ingenuity and inventive fertility" of the author.

Finally, Scott sees his characters and the narrative action, and encourages his readers to see both, not only as a colorful portrait of an exciting time but also as representative of the larger struggle between two races and cultures whose civil strife will bring about a new order. His decision to expand beyond the Scottish novels and focus also on England did not reflect a basic change in his attitude toward human character. Tradition and progress maintained their importance in his analysis of human evolution, particularly the conflict between the past heroic ideal and the present industrial society. In *Ivanhoe* Scott develops the theme of national unity, fleshing it out largely in three unforgettable scenes—the Ashby tournament, the siege of Torquilstone, and the Templestowe trial. By unifying both cultures under a banner of law and order, Scott suggests the final failure of chivalry and its heroic code. A new nation, England, takes form as the difficult passage from a romantic, heroic era to a period of tenuous optimism and inconclusive progress is begun. And it is this situation that is germane today; *Ivanhoe,* like most important literature, expresses an unflinching moral realism, while its philosophical and social content reveals eternal forces in constant struggle between the requirements of order and freedom, of law and individuality, of established procedure and the drive for a new world order.

3

The Critics and *Ivanhoe*

The history of the criticism of *Ivanhoe* may stand as an example of one of the liveliest and most diverse receptions given any novel in English fiction. From the first reviews in February 1820—"We do not recollect perusing any work of Walter Scott's that has afforded us more pleasure than the present"[2]—the critics seemed as happy with the novel as the reading public. When disapproval did surface, it was so guarded that the reviewer's true attitude could be discovered only after quite careful reading: "It [*Ivanhoe*] contains more information of a certain kind . . . is richer in antiquarian details, than perhaps any other; but it has less of verisimilitude, and makes a much more evanescent, if not a less vivid impression upon the reader's fantasy" (*CH*, 188).

Other critics suggested the experimental nature of the work—as a romance—revealed the clever intentions of the author, but at least some critics have judged *Ivanhoe* a failure. A romance writer, as one reviewer explains, cannot expect his readers to hover perpetually between history and romance without receiving the true character of either. Scott's ready answer, delivered by his fictional antiquarian editor Laurence Templeton in the novel's dedicatory epistle, became the banner explanation for historical romance writers who felt the necessity of defending their methods: "I neither can nor do pretend to the observation of complete accuracy . . . [and] I have in no respect exceeded the fair license due to the author of a fortuitous composition."[3]

Scott suggests, and his early critics agree on, as do a number of recent scholars, different requirements for judging *Ivanhoe*. No longer can the public judge a novel solely according to realistic standards as a "stenographic transcription of society," while ignoring its romantic elements. New critical judgment must come to terms with its idealizing, symbolic, and affective characteristics or lose any notion of what is meant by the romance narrative. Critics who ignore Scott's intentions and condemn *Ivanhoe* for its lack of utilitarian virtue and minimal sociological realism mistake his attempt for something else and thus find it wanting.

Coleridge's response to the novel defines this "lack of virtue" in its earliest form. While admitting to never having read the entire novel, he complains first of the "feeble interest excited by Rowena" but finds "the want of any one predominant interest aggravated by the want of any one continuous thread of events" a "grievous defect" (*CH*, 182). The reviewer for the *Eclectic Review* (June 1820) made a similar complaint, focusing on the contrasts inherent in history and romance. Neither critic willingly admits that the struggle of the two cultures, Norman and Saxon (or modern and ancient), can have any deep and lasting interest for the reader. Instead, the assumption is that *Ivanhoe* may amuse, but it requires no thought and excites no deep emotions. As harsh as this criticism was, it was nonetheless pervasive. Yet it remained a minority response, with the majority of critics praising the extensive description and Scott's decision in turning to England for his subject.

During the nineteenth century the popularity, and critical opinion, of the Waverley Novels (as Scott's collected novels were known) remained relatively stable. With the various cultural, political, social, regional, and gender conflicts of the late Victorian period, however, the reading public began slowly drifting away. From the 1880s to the 1980s, Scott's reputation suffered a serious decline, epitomized best in E. M. Forster's attack in *Aspects of the Novel* (1927). Scott can tell a story, Forster says, but he lacks passion, "he only has a temperate heart."[4]

How does this view square with the contemporary idea that *Ivanhoe,* and Scott's other medieval novels, should be recognized as a subset of the Waverley Novels, revealing affinities more with romance than with the psychological novel? Forster searches for a type of passion that would run counter to the novel's premise: Scott stylizes his characters, polarizing their values and arranging both in a symmetrical plot.[5]

For the last half century and more, many critics have returned to the Waverley Novels with new interest and pleasure. Jane Millgate's *Walter Scott: The Making of the Novelist* (1984) finds recent attempts at rescuing Scott from the collected fiction have made a common error. Most often these discussions concentrate on the "best" Scottish novels—*Waverley* (1814), *Rob Roy* (1817), *The Heart of Midlothian* (1818), *The Bride of Lammermoor* (1819), and *Redgauntlet* (1824). By selecting such a group under one theme, their historical Scottishness, one loses "those insights that derive from the awareness of sequence and interconnection as factors in both the genesis and reception of the novels as first published."[6] Millgate acknowledges *Ivanhoe* as a major shift in historical focus but not as a break with the established pattern. Scott, she finds, disliked innovation and made changes only when precedent supported his plans. When he signalled the change in focus by having the novels from *Waverley* to *A Legend of Montrose* (1819) reissued as *The Novels and Tales of the Author of Waverley* in the same year of *Ivanhoe*'s publication, Scott announced a shift in the balance between historical realism and romance in the collected fiction.

Millgate refers quite enticingly to *Ivanhoe*'s "Tintoesque pictorialism and the patterned simplicities of its highly stylized narrative procedures" (191). These elements, she believes, mark a delicate change in Scott's balance of historical realism and romance design. To praise Scott for his ability to imitate nature, especially its passion and color, acknowledges a point of view shared by many critics. Though this quality is not mentioned with the high regard it once was; nonetheless, Scott does work like Titian, particularly his later paintings, where "with great patches of color . . . they cannot be seen near, but at a distance they look perfect."[7]

A frequently noted anomaly in the criticism of *Ivanhoe* is that one generation may call it "a wretched abortion" and the next find the novel "an arrival, not a departure." Judith Wilt's *Secret Leaves: The Novels of Walter Scott* (1985) intends to restore Scott to his rightful position as one of the great imaginative geniuses of the nineteenth century. She rediscovers the coherence, the moral and epistemological complexity, and artistry of his novels by thematically reading them in pairs. Using such symbolic motifs as love and hate, enthusiasm and reason, destiny and choice, romance and realism, she discusses language, gender, and the unconscious "subversions" in Scott's novels. Chapter 1 examines the continuity of theme, image, and technique between an early Scottish novel and a later "medieval" one. Her argument is that if *Waverley* was a beginning, then *Ivanhoe* must serve as a rebeginning. Her thesis is typical of the prevailing current interpretation of the novel.[8]

Ivanhoe, Wilt avers, is the central piece of evidence for Scott's transition from Scotch-based, race-identified reality to another aesthetic, that of national myth making (the priest—King—Robin Hood myth). *Waverley*, Scott's first novel, has key images and ideas reflecting usurpation and its attendant forms, kidnapping, borrowing, disguising, and imposture. "These illegitimate actions enable the construction of those modern fictions of legitimacy, the state and the self" (Wilt, 20). If *Waverley* proposes how we might understand the ebb and flow of history, at least in Scotland, and by association Western Europe, his ninth novel, *Ivanhoe*, might logically suggest a repetition and an extension of similar historical-political ideas. The old critical orthodoxy separating the medieval (or English and continental) novels from the Scotch novels remains self-defeating; the Waverley Novels support with good assurance a central and concurrent thesis.

Francis R. Hart's *Scott's Novels: The Plotting of Historical Survival* (1966), anticipating Wilt, argues convincingly that Scott had found new freedom with *Ivanhoe* since it permitted further progress toward explaining premodern European history. Its 600-year distance and remoteness of subject matter offered greater opportunities for "symbolic renderings."[9] This complexity provides historical associations with *Waverley*, since both books reveal their respective epochs by employing cultural tensions and "embodying crisis and transformation" in character relationships. Scott's ability to creatively combine recognizable human experience with social and political issues dramatically heightens his reconstruction of history.

Millgate, Wilt, Hart, and other contemporary critics have found the dismissive attitudes of early and mid-twentieth-century critics to be rather ingenious (though more often obvious) efforts at denigrating the entire Scott canon by separating *Ivanhoe* from the Waverley pattern. To suggest the novel's simplicity became the single, most effective means of reducing its importance: a romance with no coherent past milieu; a history unimaginatively grounded in an artificial human experience; an English story written to widen the popularity of a Scottish regionalist. A realization once lost, and now recently recovered, suggests the novel's complexity, its contradictory interpretations. If generations of readers found the book's chivalry and adventure satisfying and numerous others noted its antichivalric attitude, the result must be a book of greater depth than most critics have been willing to admit or understand.

The contemporary debates on Scott have produced a rich and enthusiastic reassessment of the writer. The main lines of development in modern criticism, usually considered as literary paradigms, have swirled about *Ivanhoe*. Often the most effective in stimulating readers to reassess the novel have been the historical, feminist, and reader-response approaches.

A historical approach to *Ivanhoe* describes the novel as a rereading of the history of the early nineteenth century. Successful historical criticism, like Marilyn Butler's *Romantics, Rebels, and Reactionaries* (1982), suggests quite convincingly that Scott's subject in his novel is revolution. It seems reasonable to bring out in this study the generally positive qualities of revolt as background to *Ivanhoe*. This projects the historical process itself as a kind of author who asks readers to understand how a historical moment produced a particular literary response. The sequences of history that Scott describes in his fictional Middle Ages make comprehensible his own time, a way of knowing his world.

The urgency of the desire to understand literature from its historical context has encouraged literary critics to look beyond formalist esthetics to the context of power relations. This approach has natural affinities with feminist criticism that urges the acceptance of historical compromise, an acceptance of a power shift from male to female. Though Scott does not easily come to my mind as a writer who assisted the development of a feminist esthetic, he did advance the recognition of women as belonging in culture rather than being outside of it. *Ivanhoe,* for example, shows clearly the dominance of the patriarchal culture in which a male-dominated social discourse allows various misogynist practices to occur. As improbable as it may seem, Scott has his dark heroine, Rebecca, speak with authority against those fathers in the narrative who oppress humanity. He begins the important process of asking questions, demanding that new attention be paid to all relationships in private and public life, especially those bearing on culture and power, female and male.

Examining the patterns of behavior in the characters of *Ivanhoe* and these patterns in relation to the moral, social, and political principles identified in the shape of the novel's action and critical scenes, the reader starts a process of filling in the narrative gaps. Wolfgang Iser's studies of reader-oriented practices—*The Act of Reading* (1978) and *Prospecting: From Reader Response to Literary Anthropology* (1989)— suggest the reader must fill in or make up details or connections within a story. All stories contain such gaps, and the text is only complete when the reader's experience finishes the building of structure. For our purposes one might begin answering the question of whether *Ivanhoe*-Scott orchestrates the reader's participation or the reader virtually writes the novel by filling in gaps without any pressure from the novelist. Reader-response criticism continues struggling with this dilemma; yet whatever the answer may be, our understanding of *Ivanhoe* can only profit from studying how the reader interacts with the work in order to interpret the text.

A READING

4

Ivanhoe: The Mask of Chivalry

Lady Louisa Stuart wrote to her friend Walter Scott on 16 January 1820 that she and her family had been reading "an odd new kind of book called Ivanhoe."[10] Curiously captivated by her favorite novelist's shift from Scottish concerns, Lady Stuart struggled to understand why, though, "The interest of it, indeed, is most powerful; few things in prose or verse seize upon one's mind so strongly." Scott's earliest technique of blending language, literature, and history had found ready acceptance with the reading public. Now, in the novels of the 1820s, he had moved to treat issues of social and cultural conflict in medieval England and on the Continent. His readers would soon realize that the issues remained the same; Scott was concerned with the future of British society.

Whatever the setting or the cultural origin of his characters, Scott maintained a constancy of vision (for which he is given little credit). Purposefully centering his narrative on the relation of the individual to the dynamic of history, he examined the dangers in the democratic spirit directing itself against the rigidity of a monarchist society. The hero, defined by his free manliness and aggressive spirit of independence, opposes competition in society: he serves as Scott's point of reference. The irony, of course, was that society needed such a figure's leadership and courage to secure stability and establish justice. The heroic ideal simultaneously comprised both an innate challenge to government and a commitment to social justice. It implied the constructive impulse for rebuilding a new society.

Scott's own Tory politics, as fashionably understood, separated him in some important aspects from those of his countrymen who kept to the tenets of Scots literature. Scots characteristically took pleasure in arguing their individual points of view; they prized the democratic spirit. Often the only result was disagreement, but a rugged individualism persevered. Scott cannot suppress his confidence in the common man's preservation of society, his mistrust of enthusiasm, his preference for the middle way, and his soberness of judgment. Whatever his particular political response, Scott's impulse was always to reconcile factions. Though *Ivanhoe*, at first glance, has everything to do with war and the clash of armies, its true center can be seen in Scott's desire for cohesiveness and union between Norman and Saxon, or English and Scotch.

If it is true that Scott was allegorizing contemporary political events and also writing a book embodying quite private values, he had decided on an uncommon approach: *Ivanhoe* would be a chivalric romance. What the implications of this decision were and how Scott managed to conceive of such a work require more explanation, for misunderstandings arising from both have caused no end of difficulties for critics and readers alike. What makes *Ivanhoe* difficult, I would argue, is also what makes it great: its skillful arrangement of improbabilities, impossibilities, and coincidences. All have caused readers brought up on the realistic fiction of Henry Fielding and Tobias George Smollett considerable distress. Accusations usually directed at Scott or Ivanhoe, as if the book somehow came to life without an author, suggest that the considerable number of historical inaccuracies render the novel unhistorical and thus unworthy of any further attention. Scott, who was a superb historian, could produce historical novels; his works from *Waverley* to *Redgauntlet* prove as much. But the key in *Ivanhoe* is his bent for the fantastic. Scott makes quite clear early in the novel when defending the Templars' African slaves, "But neither will I allow that the author of a modern antique romance is obliged to confine himself to the introduction of those manners only which can be proved to have absolutely existed in the times he is depicting, so that he restrain himself to such as are plausible and natural, and contain no obvious anachronism"(551–52). Scott has considerable fascination for antiquarian customs, culture, and language but refuses, quite explicitly, to limit his novel to only objective historical and cultural relativities.

Scott, who hoped for a popular book, was responding at least partially to the Gothic vogue in fiction. From Horace Walpole's *The Castle of Otranto* (1764) and its host of imitators, including Clara Reeve's *The Old English Baron* (1777), Ann Radcliffe's *The Mysteries of Udolpho* (1794), and Matthew Lewis's *The Monk* (1795), the Gothic transformation gave readers, bored by the realistic novel's commitment to propriety, an escape from the distressing complexities of the present. Walpole wrote "in defiance of actors, rulers and philosophers," and Scott was doing something rather similar; he seized the moment for embracing fantasy while still adhering to the truth. If *Ivanhoe* is confusing, it is because Scott would not do what the public has often required of its artists—conform. He must write history or romance; he must treat his subjects realistically or fantastically, but never both simultaneously. To his credit, Scott wrote a book we cannot dismiss, not because of its simplicity but because of its complexity.

Ivanhoe may have been in Scott's mind totally fantastic, but his early readers thought they were seeing the Middle Ages reincarnated. What he intended was subtle, and this intention is clear in his introduction and the dedicatory epistle to the novel. These opening sections reveal Scott's intention as a creator of myth, romance, and symbol. If Marilyn Butler is correct, Scott "could convey a portrait of contemporary society, and at the same time represent as central the plight of individuals whose lives were caught up in an impersonal mechanism."[11]

By constructing elaborate explanations of his purpose in *Ivanhoe*, Scott was continuing his use of pseudonyms, a practice begun early in his career when he resorted to publishing *Waverley* anonymously. His reasons for secrecy were often hidden behind his public (at least to his publishers) and his private (journals) proclamations. Apparently, he originally worried that his efforts as a novelist would fail and ruin his reputation in the world as a poet. Later, when *Waverley* became a great popular success, Scott said he had no need of the public's gratitude since he had earlier won it. What is more likely and more in keeping with his personality is that Scott took mischievous enjoyment in keeping a secret at the expense of his friends and the general public. He enjoyed himself further as the author of *Waverley* with *Guy Mannering* in 1815, then *The Antiquary* in 1816.

Later in 1816 he offered *Tales of My Landlord, First Series*, the group title of two novels, as the work of an unknown country schoolteacher. But the unknown had a rival. The novels—*The Black Dwarf, Old Mortality*—had been edited, according to the joke, with expertise by Jedediah Cleishbotham of Gandercleuch, translated from the Scots as Jedediah Thwackass of Gander's Hollow. Absurd as it was, the public was delighted whether Scott wrote as the author of the *Waverley Novels* or as a rustic schoolmaster from Gander's Hollow. After changing publishers once again, Scott decided for his next novel, *Rob Roy* (1817), not to continue with Jedediah, returning instead to the unknown Author. This would heighten the competition between the two supposed writers.

In the meantime Scott had continued his practice of writing elaborate prefaces or introductions (supposedly written by these fictional personas) with the intent of setting a tone or mood for the narrative. His intention was to reinvoke the atmosphere of an earlier time, when events seemed to move more slowly and the storyteller could relate a tale leisurely and expansively. For Scott, the concern of joining history with fiction and summoning the reader's full powers of discovery within the world of his novel remained paramount.

The Heart of Midlothian (1818), the continuation of the "Tales of My Landlord" series, advances his discussion of Scottish history, both national and parochial, to a higher level. Finally, in 1819, with *The Bride of Lammermoor* and *A Legend of Montrose*, the Landlord series was completed with this third group of novels. In each case, prefatory material written by the fictional persona Jedediah suggests the tales and legends were collected with the help of another, but more "simple," fellow, one who lacked the experience or world view of

Cleishbotham. The intent remained on the theme of discovery, whereby the reader is given a chance, through reading artless tales of simple folk as told from a sophisticated point of view, to recognize the deficiencies of his own existence and the possible solutions for counterbalancing them.

The content and form of these introductions, while fictive, often has quite historical or real goals, calculated to animate history in the reader's mind. In *Ivanhoe*, Scott became the pompous Laurence Templeton writing an "Epistle" to the Rev. Dr. Dryasdust as a humorous way of sharpening the curiosity and stimulating the excitement of his readers. Typical of his writing habits, Scott explains quite coherently in these essays far more than the modern reader, who is quite understandably bored by the joke, will willingly permit.

Whatever our initial response to *Ivanhoe*, one can see within the first paragraphs of the epistle what Scott has in mind and why. He confirms the innovative character of the new novel while discreetly assuring readers of his attachment to sane human feelings, no matter the "peculiar state of society." Evidence comes in his references to the characters, Oldbuck of Monkbarns and Sir Arthur Wardour of *The Antiquary* (1816), and in the comparison of Robin Hood with Rob Roy (the outlaw of his 1818 novel). While moving to shift the balance of historical realism and Gothic fantasy, Scott recalls his earlier purpose in the Scottish novels to "excite an interest for the traditions and manners . . . of our poorer and less celebrated neighbors" (522). Writing as the Englishman Templeton, Scott plays upon the interest all Britons, all Europeans for that matter, took in James Macpherson's *Poems of Ossian* (1760–63) and in the resulting controversy over its authenticity as a national epic. Responding to earlier criticisms of his novels, he willingly admits to employing "like a second M'Pherson the antiquarian stories which lay scattered around him" (522), and when it became necessary supplying recent events, real characters, and even real names. Scott acknowledges in bold terms his practicing a mixed form of fiction.

Such an effort needs further clarification, however; he seeks to explain the curious differences facing a narrator of Scottish society as opposed to one who narrates the history of England. "To match an

English and Scottish author in the rival task of embodying and reviving the traditions of their respective countries would be . . . in the highest degree unequal and unjust" (523). The nature of the English author's task requires an ambitious writer who, knowing his source material is a collection of "dry, sapless, mouldering, and disjointed bones," persists anyway. He has none of the Scot's advantages, especially the recent history of Scotland's modern society, which provides the historian with living witnesses to these events. The narrator of *Ivanhoe* has as a starting point musty records and chronicles in which all "interesting details" have been suppressed in order to expound moral norms. Scott builds, certainly, a compelling case for how he, or any author possessed of the talent and intuitive skill, might rise above such limitations. Now, Scott admits that his intention soon turned away from conventionally relating history as if it were lifeless. The task of the novelist, as he realized, must be one of translating history into terms relevant for the reader.[12] Since the possibility of human reactions to a historical event are limitless, the novelist may employ this diversification to successfully relate historical reality.

Scott's break with the old novel forms began earlier, in *Waverley*, and in thinking about *Ivanhoe*, he advanced the argument further. To start with, he altered the definition of antiquary to meet his own personal experience. He had done the toilsome research necessary for historical accuracy in completing Joseph Strutt's posthumous novel *Queenhoo Hall* (1807), but had realized the danger of relying solely on historical fact without "the playful fascination . . . of intermingling fiction with truth" (526). The lesson learned from that failure becomes a critical element for *Ivanhoe*. "I neither can nor do pretend to the observation of complete accuracy," nor will I "confine myself within the limits of the periods in which my story is laid" (526).

Templeton, as "author" of *Ivanhoe*, adopts a modest tone when speaking to the rigid antiquarian, Dr. Dryasdust. Only by urging cautiously that blending fiction with history can cause no harm does he stand a chance of convincing this authority figure. Begging the triviality of his tale as an apology for the scarcity of the historical evidence on the period, his final appeal is as one realist to another. While arguing the necessity for artistic license, Templeton addresses the issue of the public's response to *Ivanhoe*, comparing it with the Antoine Galland's translation of the *Arabian Tales*. "The tales were eminently better fitted for the European market . . . and [met with] an unrivaled degree of public favour [when] the manners and style had been . . . familiarized to the feelings and habits of the Western reader" (527). Scott, through his narrator, goes on developing this point again and again with references as diverse as translating Chaucer from Middle English to criticizing Chatterton for creating an injudicious dialect for his fabrication, the Rowley poems.[13] Certainly the artist must retain his freedom of choice in adapting an ancient tale for its modern readers. Whatever the alterations made in translating ancient manners and speech, modern readers have the consolation of knowing they share a common nature with their ancient ancestors.

Another quality evident in Templeton's ornate argument involves Scott's unending concern for the success or failure of his novels. Characteristically, the *Ivanhoe* narrator assures his readers — "the multitudes who will, I trust, devour this book with avidity" — that every effort has been taken in reducing "the repulsive dryness of mere antiquity" (527). To this point, Scott has taken every precaution against limiting the popularity of *Ivanhoe*. The decision of relying on a fictional narrator, once again, and now citing Sir Arthur Wardour's mythical manuscript as his primary source, compounds the risk.

Yet Scott treats such risk in a consistent manner; in *The Antiquary* Sir Arthur Wardour meditates on the loss of his estate and debtor's prison after another one of his dangerous financial schemes collapses. One imagines how Scott doubted the potential success of *Ivanhoe*, how his risky decision to break with Scottish themes and turn to English history might have been a grand mistake. His metaphor of the risky business enterprise is clarified in *Rob Roy*: "who embarks on that fickle sea, requires to possess the skill of the pilot and the fortitude of the navigator, and often all may be wrecked . . . unless the gales of fortune breathe in his favour."[14]

Scott hazards his reputation and fortune on what he calls this "presumptuous attempt to frame for myself a minstrel coronet partly out of pearls of pure antiquity, and partly from . . . paste" (531). The notion of recreating the past remains his basic principle, and its historical reality can only be realized by linking it with the present in terms conceivable for the modern reader. Francis Hart explains the paradigm: "the new figure who often emerges at the end of a *Waverley* Novel . . . is a restorer who takes over the old estate and returns it . . . in a form essentially true to the lost tradition." [15]

Ivanhoe represents a similar ideological approach as far as the nine *Waverley* novels before it, but replicating this pattern repeatedly, as Scott suggests in the introduction (536), could also prove fatal. His new direction becomes one of imaginative transferral from a particular class of subjects, whose novelty and charm were in danger of being exhausted, to new materials, tempered in the ancient values, but exhibiting considerably new freedoms. The legitimacy of *Ivanhoe* depends on Scott's fictitious consistency, or simply the principle of imitating history. The truth of historical reality is brought to life in the fictional environment; thus, the balance of invention and truth maintains the novel's credibility. Scott creates in *Ivanhoe*, and his best novels, the illusion of historical reality without restricting that reality to the fictional scenario he created.

5

A Broken Path

In commenting on Mark Twain's famous opinion of Scott as one who "comes with his enchantments . . . and checks this wave of progress . . . sets the world in love with dreams and phantoms," a recent critic suggests we have been viewing an "interesting psychodrama of sublimation and misreading."[16] The plight of Scott, and *Ivanhoe* in particular, has been how we, the living, might understand the work of a dead man whose most popular book continues to ward off death. This dilemma has forced Scott's modern readers into redefining the nature of *Ivanhoe*'s effect. Why is it and how is it defensible to suggest, as does Judith Wilt, that this novel is "the key text"? Without fully representing her subtle and extensive argument, one might see some important Victorian writers, Thackeray and Thomas Carlyle among them, as well as the twentieth-century novelists Joseph Conrad, Ford Madox Ford, and E. M. Forster, as quite heavily indebted to Scott (Wilt 1981, 460). His notion of the hero and heroism, in addition to his moral intensity and commitment to truth, anticipate important dimensions of their works.

Ivanhoe may serve as the "key" for later writers if we recognize that for Scott's contemporaries there was only one other text,

Waverley, that had primacy. Both novels examine the truth of human nature, "where young men and women fight for identity on the slippery interface between destiny and choice, lusting and desire, contrivance and spontaneity" (Wilt 1981, 461). Scott's technique for establishing this tension and exploring its moral complexity is seen in the novel's balanced structure. Unsettling as it may seem to the traditional view of *Ivanhoe,* Scott was not simply constructing the novel around several actions or incidents (as is so often argued) hoping only to maintain the reader's interest. If this intention were his sole purpose then a serious reader might ignore the novel, or read it as a simple curio of early nineteenth-century literature. What may lend credence even to this sort of reading, however, is Scott's ability to arouse our interest in action, characters, and coincidence for their own sake, thus deceiving us into believing that it is all rainbow and no gravity. The great virtue of *Ivanhoe* is that we become caught up in the adventure, even as the novel provides ample cause for our contemplation of the human experience, and in quite significant ways.

When Scott adopted the ethic of romance, he revealed what Northrop Frye calls a capacity to suggest implicit mythical patterns in a world more closely associated with human experience.[17] *Ivanhoe* organizes itself in a series of myths or mythical patterns, not in a series of causally connected incidents. Chapters 1–18 form a carefully designed presentation, leading to a mythic conclusion concerning the nature of heroism. In particular Scott explores the nature of the self-doubting hero ("the changeling protagonist"), Wilfred of *Ivanhoe,* and his battle with the three "fathers" (Cedric, John, and Richard) on his return home. Chapters 19–33 embody the myth of nationhood, the progress of culture, the dying out of feudalism, and the emergence of a national society. The siege of Torquilstone, for all its exciting improbability and energy, has its real significance as a metaphor of transformation as a group of individuals band together serving a peaceful, stable society. Finally, chapters 34–44 define the ultimate competition between romance and real life, the emotional and the intellectual, by exploring the myth of the disinherited. Scott uses myth as a way of explaining the structural principles of the novel. In the most well-known example of the emotion versus the rational, *Ivanhoe* does not marry his soul mate, Rebecca, in the end; reversing his sympathies, he instead marries Rowena. As he was well aware, romance, concerning itself primarily with an idealized world, need not achieve plausibility or "realism." The distinction Scott insisted upon between novel and romance applies exactly to *Ivanhoe.* The inaccessibility of the Middle Ages demanded the reader's acceptance of an act of faith or suspension of disbelief.

Ivanhoe exists as a stylized figure that can reflect, in Frye's terms, a subjective intensity, "something nihilistic and untamable." Exploring this notion of Ivanhoe's character provides fascinating possibilities when we balance it against the traditional romance figure, idealizing heroism, loyalty, mercy, and justice. Cedric, who must serve as an unwilling host to a group of traveling Normans, thinks of his son's consuming emotions, exclaiming "Ah, Wilfred, Wilfred . . . coulds't thou have ruled thine unreasonable passion, thy father had not left in his age like the solitary oak that throws out its shattered and unprotected branches against the full sweep of the tempest!"(36).

Scott heightens the significance here between Saxon and Norman by evoking the world adumbrated in the *Poems of Ossian,* verse tales embracing the myths of Scott's Celtic culture. The regret, mourning, sense of loss—familiar traits of Ossianic poetry—all appear here in a rhythm of lament, Cedric's grand remonstrance against the erosion of his world. The father mourns his son's apparent unwillingness to recognize the horror of what the new Norman world represents. Ivanhoe apparently rejects his father's definition of duty, in effect casting out the natural, the "realistic," father, and replacing him with a new father, the romantic and impractical King Richard, whom he has followed on the Crusade. Society and the individual reflect the corrupt atmosphere: chaos, destruction, and ruin are rampant.

ENCOUNTER IN THE GREEN WORLD

The entire opening section of *Ivanhoe* embodies conflict, beginning early with the passage of the Normans, led by the corrupt churchman Prior Aymer and his sinister companion the Knight Templar Brian Bois-Guilbert, through Sherwood Forest en route to Rotherwood. These alien invaders come upon the rude Saxons, Gurth and Wamba, who are one with the landscape, "partaking . . . of that wild and rustic character which belonged to the woodlands" (11). For all their apparent harmony with the natural surroundings ("the green world"), the two Saxons remain pathetic, even defeated figures. Scott's language in describing their emotions and feelings reveals quite effectively their state: "sad and sullen," "deep source of defection," "apathy," "sullen dependency, a sense of oppression." Only the merest suggestion of a zest for life and freedom counters the earlier words; Gurth possesses a "fire which occasionally sparkled in his red eye," and Wamba exhibits "a sort of vacant curiosity and fidgety impatience" (13). The process of growth seems to have stopped—we come upon the story (of which Scott's epigraph from the *Odyssey* is suggestive) at a kind of nadir where stability seems quite impossible, where the hero hides from those who know him and will shortly refer to himself as the "disinherited Knight."

Significant, too, is the activity of Wamba and Gurth, who search for a lost herd of swine with another victim of the current despair, the "limping lurcher," their dog Fangs, disabled according to Norman Forest law. (Claws on the right foot are removed, preventing the dog from chasing and scattering the deer herd.) As a thunderstorm approaches, symbolic of nature's unpredictability, the two men debate the value of collecting the scattered animals: "leave the herd to their destiny, which, whether they meet with bands of travelling soldiers, or of outlaws, or of wandering pilgrims, can be little else than to be converted into Normans" (14). Wamba, cynical about the chances of these "innocent lambs," cannot only sense the coming conflict but also its participants: the Norman knights, Robin Hood and his men; and the Crusaders, Ivanhoe and Richard.

An underlying motive introduced in the Wamba-Gurth portrait, and often overlooked by readers, is the moral superiority of real property. Scott's imagination, his deepest emotions, as Alexander Welsh explains, had often responded to the sacredness of property in the *Waverley* Novels.[18] The *Ivanhoe* scenario further reflects this force of property, its economic influence on the society. The Norman nobles oppress their weaker neighbors, the Saxons, first with the sword and later, more significantly, through a series of quasi-legal actions that reduce the defeated English to servitude while seizing, or threatening to seize, their lands. Gurth speaks candidly about his condition: "little is left to us but the air we breathe, and that . . . solely for the purpose of enabling us to endure the tasks they lay upon our shoulders" (15).

The question becomes what has been lost, and its corollary—what is the nature of this loss. Scott suggests the loss of two species of property whose characteristics are quite different. The first class of property contains moral, ethical concerns. Since property is a concept, distinct from the possession or use of a thing, the rights to employ some object or land do not exist in the object itself. Property is better understood as a nonspecific relationship between things and persons. Among certain of Scott's contemporaries, property suggested only the quality of possession, while introducing the idea of a rival for the object. The passivity of property depends on recognizing that its rights impose obligations on others, "expresses what *ought* to be occupied or used by whom, and not merely the fact of occupation" (Welsh, 96). These ethical statements have more clarity when associated with the notion of law; as far as Scott was concerned, any theory of property must answer to the actual situation of society. Thus property promotes and represents order within the society as persons respond to the community's laws by accepting the boundary lines of property. Gurth and Wamba, as Cedric's bondsmen and his property, are in the excellent position of judging to what degree their owner's property has suffered under Norman rule. The Norman civil government should adhere to the principle that the preservation of property is the chief end of a commonwealth. If it violates this absolute law, the government is corrupt and cannot stand: "property is both the cause and best defense of civil society" (Welsh, 102).

Scott's philosophy toward property had been influenced by Adam Smith and John Locke, but he also held a thoroughly realistic view. Happiness or success, he often proved, can be suitably defined through the possession of material wealth. He understood that property marked the individual's social worth. The decision to buy Abbotsford was the fulfillment of Scott's dream of building "a little cottage where he could gather his family around his own fireside under the shelter of his own rooftree."[19] Since the original buildings were unattractive and the grounds quite bare, Scott was first attracted to the setting, the features and shape of the land. He intended to plant trees, hundreds of oaks and chestnuts, in which he might compose a new "landscape of living trunks and leaves clothing the swelling curves . . . of the earth itself" (Johnson, 371). More than making his own success, he revised the significance of "the poet who has bought himself a farm." By associating himself with the land, he might now begin cultivating it (at least in trees), making fertile and productive what had been barren.

Though Scott is far from becoming a farmer in the usual sense of the word, he does cherish the social achievement of becoming purposefully reunited with the land. Any threat to this bond, especially in his fiction, is treated as a significant narrative theme. As we have shown, the social atmosphere in *Ivanhoe* is often explained metaphorically, and Scott's treatment of the franklins, freeholders who often owned extensive property, suggests his extended views on property. Anticipating our introduction to Gurth and Wamba, and particularly Cedric of Rotherwood, Scott recalls the law and spirit of the English constitution protecting the independence of the franklins. The dangerous actions of "petty kings" (used interchangeably with "feudal tyranny," "ambitions of their protector[s]," "oppression . . . by the great barons") will sacrifice the franklins' independence (8). The Normans' lawless conduct will destroy the franklin's property, the measure of their social worth as well as the criterion of their citizenship.

For Scott the equation of property with political responsibility remains central to an understanding of the forest metaphor connecting his comments on the franklins with the entrance of Gurth and Wamba. The sun sets on the magnificence and rich variety of the forest: "hundreds of broad-headed, short-stemmed, wide-branched oaks, which had witnessed perhaps the stately march of the Roman soldiery, flung their gnarled arms over a thick carpet . . . in some places they were intermingled with beeches, hollies, and copsewoods . . . forming long sweeping vistas in the intricacy of which the eye delights" (10). With this enchanting description Scott launches this complex vision for an emerging civil society. The potential for peace and security among humankind is suggested in the extensive variety of trees coexisting in a mutually conducive environment. The world of the forest has withstood the earlier Roman invaders and remained unchanged. The natural law that governs and secures the forest can encourage a resurgence of human society. The Saxon franklins, yeomen, and laborers (bondsmen), as well as those Norman barons and knights who refuse to manipulate the law falsely, are inextricably united in the property belonging to the King. From such a kingly estate, civil society is created. When the King is weak or displaced by a scheming villain (Prince John), the "long sweeping vistas" of property can be stolen away from the proper owners: the result produces disorder and civil war.

Scott once again relies on a subordinate character to emphasize this essential point, when Gurth, sensing the Templar's self-aggrandizing motives, refuses to show the Normans the path to Rotherwood. "I know not if I should show the way to my master's house to those who demand as a right the shelter which most are fain to ask as a favour" (24). Here Scott combines two sorts of villain effectively (this arrangement, Welsh explains, is not typical in the *Waverley* Novels). The Templar is an agent of evil and riot, while also a self-acquiring rogue, like Prince John, except his real target, Rebecca, marks his ambition as sexual, not territorial.

Scott closes this early chapter while recalling for the reader the image of Odysseus returning to reclaim his home—he does not mention Ivanhoe except by referring to what will become the prevalent heroic symbol of the novel and the disinherited knight, the oak tree. They "creak with their great boughs as if announcing a tempest," warning all who would listen that "the night will be fearful" (16). The romance of the hero returning, taking back his possessions and purging his home of corruption, is the relevant theme of the novel's opening section. The *mythos* (Frye's term) or argument sets the boundaries for the conflict between the culture and the individual—both must effect change and be changed themselves by the experience.

APPROACHING ROTHERWOOD

With the coming of darkness, the Normans appear symbolically representative of the twin poles of medieval life, the Church and the Court, in the characters of Prior Aymer, a Cistercian monk, and Brian De

Bois-Gilbert, a Knight-Templar and ex-Crusader. Not surprisingly, they are lost, certainly in a spiritual sense; both men exhibit degenerate spirits, associated in Scott's mind with their overcivilized backgrounds. Aymer and Bois-Guilbert may have been born nobles, but their lives anticipate a brand of villainy quite unnatural in the green world of the Forest. In need of "harborage" and "hospitality" the Normans, each in his own ignorance, struggle with Wamba and Gurth for knowledge of a path to a home (sanctuary) willing to receive them. Bois-Guilbert demands answers from the Saxons who in his mind are no better than slaves; Aymer bribes and wheedles answers using money and false compliments. Since they ask questions inhospitably, they receive lies as answers. Gurth's most telling comment—"the road will be uneasy to find" (24)—does not have a salutary effect on the invaders who ignore this bit of native wisdom.

These Normans who search for security from the approaching (metaphorical) storm lack the vision and imagination to recognize the truth, even in its primitive form. The antagonists—the Saxons, who live in harmony with their world, and these Normans, who live in ignorant disrespect of their surroundings—are clearly drawn. Now it remains to the hero to promote understanding, conciliation, and compromise; yet he has not appeared, though clearly the reader senses the moment is near. He must guide them all to a better understanding at Rotherwood.

Ironically, Ivanhoe too searches for sanctuary; we soon learn the hero (disguised as a palmer—a professional pilgrim to the Holy Land) knows the way to Cedric's residence, but its value to him as a refuge, a shelter, remains in doubt. Ivanhoe's disguise as a palmer permits him entry to Rotherwood according to the laws of hospitality, but as Cedric's son he would have been unwelcome. Only through the hero's power of action can he ultimately shed his disguise and reveal his true self. Though his role as a palmer suggests the character of one who searches passively for the ultimate truth, Ivanhoe does not need knight's armor before showing his assertiveness and purpose.

Scott's early theme of the quest, punctuated by conflict and resolved through a series of tests, begins with *Ivanhoe*'s almost mystical appearance; the Templar declares: "Here is someone either asleep or lying dead at the foot of this cross"(28). The hero rises from the ground, after literally falling asleep at a crossroads, in the garb of a Christian pilgrim. We can see Scott invoking the Christian myth, and thus the potential for redemption and resurrection, here between father and son. The scene serves as a prelude to the larger restoration of a new social order.

ROTHERWOOD AND THE DISINHERITED SON

It has been suggested that Scott designed his novels to offer a particular vision of a social structure and national culture. The location of Rotherwood, the seat of Cedric the Saxon, in Sherwood Forest serves as an effective vehicle for suggesting a "desirable and just" social order. The irony of Ivanhoe as a guide seems important, since he is himself at a crossroads between his Christian home (as sought in the Crusade to Palestine) and his father's home, signifying family and nationality. Rotherwood becomes the nucleus attracting two apparently different groups: the disinherited Saxon returning to his hereditary surroundings and the usurping Normans lost in conquered territory. Ivanhoe guides Bois-Guilbert and Prior Aymer, bringing "the party safely into a wider avenue than they had yet seen" (29). Rotherwood, lying hidden in the heart of the forest, embodies the natural simplicity of that world, quite in contrast to "the tall, turreted, and castelled buildings in which the Norman nobility resided" (30).

All aspects of Rotherwood suggest the Saxons live in complete harmony with the environment. The house is like one of the great forest oaks, with creatures who dwell near it living their lives according to nature's requirements. The whole, including the furniture, is constructed of oak, with the roof nearly open to the sky except for the thin planks and thatch. The earthen floor increases this sense of rude simplicity, as does the wind blowing through the house with such force that "the torches stream sideways into the air" (60). Scott extends the intimacy with the natural world as the rain often drips nearly unimpeded through the roof, falling on the inhabitants as if they were standing beneath a tree in the forest.

The nature image—the green world—achieves added focus with the appearance of Cedric, dressed in "forest green" trimmed in the fur of the grey squirrel. According to the laws of hospitality he must welcome his Norman guests, though his true feelings become obvious when he compares himself to a solitary oak caught in a violent storm. Though Ivanhoe remains unrecognized and cut off from his family, the natural imagery of trees and storms metaphorically connects and simultaneously threatens father and son. Both men are responding to the violent literal, as well as metaphorical, storm that has awakened them to yet a new threat: the extinction of their world.

Certainly, Cedric and Ivanhoe perceive the imminent destruction of their world differently. Cedric, who sees the Normans as the embodiment of pride, arrogance, and cruelty, protests against the erosion of the old native, apparently virtuous, Saxon principles. His nostalgic commitment to the past prompted his banishment of Ivanhoe and his own attachment to the imbecilic Athelstane. Cedric's Francophobia has ironically caused the old man to feel disinherited in his own land. Ivanhoe abhors the civil discord brought about by those who would destroy King Richard by supporting Prince John's abuses of authority. His first act of guiding the Normans to Rotherwood points to his role as a mediator in the novel, but his lack of success here is measured by his own early, secret departure. Rotherwood serves then as a focal point for civil discord—a testing place where Ivanhoe can size up one set of values for its practical usefulness. His decision to leave has as much to say concerning the causes of his disinheritance as it does his decision to aid the outcast Isaac. Again, Ivanhoe's heroism appears not only at the sound of trumpets on a battlefield but also during the dark, unheralded moments where he acts as peacemaker: guiding Normans to Saxon hospitality and leading the outcast Jew, Isaac, to safety. "I will guide you by the secret paths of the forest . . . and I will not leave you till you are under safe conduct" (65).

ISAAC: "THE MARGINAL MAN"

From the early chapters, Scott explores the divisions between the privileged Normans and the downtrodden Saxons, encouraging the reader's sympathy for the oppressed Cedric and his countryfolk. With the introduction of the Jew, Isaac of York, Scott compounds his analysis of estrangement and disinheritance.[20] Though Isaac is a milder Shylock—the prototypical Jew from Shakespeare's *Merchant of Venice*—with the stereotypical attributes of miser, coward, and parasite, he nonetheless represents a persecuted minority. Isaac and his daughter, Rebecca, are victims by whom Scott measures the cruelty of their Norman and Saxon oppressors and indicts the society that rejects them.

Scott initially views Isaac as the conventional money-lending "dog Jew" (as the Templar calls him), encouraging the complacent reader to believe this Jew too is surely a comic figure—a fool who is terror stricken at the thought of being attacked by the Templar's musselman slaves who would steal his money. Complicating this image of the Jew as a literary construct, Scott suggests that Isaac's usury inheres not solely in his race but is also the result of Jew-baiting by the Christians. "The obstinacy and avarice of the Jews being thus in a measure placed in opposition to the fanaticism and tyranny of [Christians], seemed to increase in proportion to the persecution with which they were visited" (70). As we note also in the frequent examples of Norman wastefulness and extravagance, one vice may stimulate another—those who would attack Isaac are more corrupt than he.

The Jew's disguise as a ludicrous old man may fool Saxons and Normans, but should not fool the reader, whom Scott has taken special pains to put on alert. When the palmer helps Isaac escape from the plot against his money and freedom, Isaac quickly notes the knight's "spurs of gold" and can interpret Ivanhoe's most heartfelt desire to seek his inheritance and recover Richard's kingdom. Isaac's response is not confusion or fear but gratitude, followed immediately by a practical solution: secure horses and armor for the pilgrim-knight. Here he uses his ducats as a weapon on behalf of Ivanhoe; symbolically, both men are the disinherited of their world, and they recognize their mutual dependence. Isaac strikes through the prejudice and fear surrounding the two races and shows Christian charity in a hostile environment where, tragically, only the disinherited knight behaves with similar virtue.

More significantly, Isaac's gift provides the tools for Ivanhoe's self-creation. As a self-doubting hero, Ivanhoe continually casts about for a purpose or at least a method for recovering the dynamic hope of his country. Since rejecting his father and his corrupted home, the hero guides, and is guided by, those who would aid his progress. The Jew, though embittered by cruelty and injustice, still retains sufficient humanity and dignity that Ivanhoe can enthusiastically rescue him. In doing so Ivanhoe begins the process of saving himself. This act, effective and uncorrupted by superficial pomp, mockingly foreshadows the brilliant, yet artificial, colors and pretense of the novel's fullest display of chivalry: the tournament of Ashby-de-la-Zouche.

THE TOURNAMENT AND ACCUMULATED DISTRESSES

Scott writes with infectious enthusiasm about the grand spectacle that "neither duty nor infirmity could keep youth or age [away] from" (75), but for all his zest he cannot restrain the powerful undercurrent of his thesis: the reality of mismanagement that has brought the nation to the point of chaos. Along with this unromantic theme he shows up the pretensions and hypocrisies of the chivalric code, its tragedies, its violence. In addition, this final scene provides an attractive setting for one of the important crises of the novel, where the hero can interact with all the opposing social forces while keeping in his own way to a middle course.

The Ashby tournament has seemed to some readers a prime example of the anticipated padding typical of a juvenile adventure story. Scott certainly exploits the picturesque potential, while simultaneously indicating the irresponsibility of its participants. No matter how much we might admire the courage of Ivanhoe, disguised as "El Desdichado," he remains an external figure—physically active but spiritually remote. Cultural groupings and hatreds reflect the condition of society, and the seating at the tournament becomes a microcosm of the nation.

As if to prove once again the corruption inherent in divisive fanaticism, Scott demonstrates the decadence of these spectators. The reference to knights and nobles in "their robes of peace" is deliberately undercut by their separation from the "substantial yeoman and burghers" and from those who have even a lesser hold on the middle rank. His ironic comment, "it was of course amongst these that the most frequent disputes for precedence occurred" (79), suggests an undercurrent of dissatisfaction in the middle class that can break out into open riot with little encouragement. The nobility remains distant and scornful of the middle class, who lack sufficient wealth and grace to set aside the private intensity of their passions for this public occasion. Scott insinuates the fundamental unwillingness of either group to embrace cooperation and progress. When one of these lesser gentry, quite poverty-stricken himself, verbally abuses Isaac and Rebecca for having done nothing more than jostle him for the good seats, the issue turns not as much on class struggle as on racial and religious prejudice.

Isaac's lack of fear stems mostly from his knowledge of the Norman character. Many of the Norman nobility, including Prince John, depend on Jews for loans of hard currency, without which they could not continue this extravagant way of life. Raising and maintaining armies in the field and squandering vast sums on developing their estates have put Richard and John into severe debt. Scott's emphasis on sound principles of economics shows the Normans in a very bad light, and by contrast the Jews' financial practices become perfectly understandable to us.

With this focus on corruption, the Norman leadership appears in its chivalric and clerical dimensions merely hypocritical—all an empty facade. Prince John, "a depraved and cowardly playboy," serves as king, while the true regent, Richard, ignores his responsibilities. John's every action prompts vice and encourages dissension. His followers embody the model of feudal aristocracy, but in its corrupt form; not one has the good of the nation in mind, only his own selfish concerns. John's faction does not respect or like him, treating him as frivolous and unimportant. Selfishness plumbs new depths in the actions of such "lawless resolutes" as the brutal Front-de-Boeuf, the larcenous Malvoisin, the foolish De Bracy, and the immoral pessimist Bois-Gilbert. To maintain this vicious faction, these Normans incite civil commotion as a cover for their various actions against the Saxons. The

Norman clergy is represented by the stylish Prior Aymer (reminiscent of Chaucer's Friar), who, when accompanying John, thinks nothing of impressing the local maidens with his fine horsemanship.

Prince John's cavalcade about the tournament grounds ends significantly with the Prince's meeting in rather quick succession two final characters, Rebecca and Robin of Locksley, who represent disinheritance and alienation, both harder to bear for the Norman persecution. Scott has earlier introduced the Saxon Rowena, who waits passively until Ivanhoe can come back for her, but with the entrance here of Rebecca, he presents an actively intelligent and highly spirited woman who is also beautiful. The pathos of disinheritance, the potential for tragedy, has increased two-fold with her arrival. Norman and Saxon alike note her obvious exotic physical attractions, "her form exquisitely symmetrical . . . the brilliancy of her eyes . . . the profusion of sable tresses . . . a lovely neck and bosom . . . a combination of loveliness" (82). Aside from these charms, it is her intellect and spirit, particularly as she speaks against chivalry or, more specifically, for human gentleness, that are Rebecca's greatest gifts. Ironically, she cannot escape the commitment and burden of her loyalty to her father and race, yet she struggles to transcend prejudice in favor of cultural continuity.

As a Saxon, Robin of Locksley is by definition already defeated and, like his kinsman Cedric, has a tragic commitment to a lost heritage. With the help of Richard and by his own considerable natural vigor and good sense, however, Robin can escape the impotence of Cedric and the unreadiness of Athelstane. Scott has resurrected in Robin a version of England's traditional folk hero—Robin Hood— who, except for eighteenth-century antiquarian interest, had not figured as a character in the national literature since Ben Jonson's pastoral drama, *The Sad Shepherd* (1637). Robin's first appearance in Ivanhoe marks him as a paradoxical figure: a yeoman of good English stock who is an outcast in his own land but whose ordinariness links him inextricably to his people.

Prince John takes immediate notice of this yeoman who refuses to be intimidated by the angry glance of his social superior. "By St. Grizzle . . . we will try his own skill, who is so ready to give his voice to the feat of others" (86). Recognizing a worthy, if not dangerous, opponent, Prince John responds to Locksley's purposeful energy by suggesting a test of arms. Scott once again broadens his concept of the hero in the novel. Not only is Ivanhoe shown, even as an outcast, more willing to protect and serve others than reclaim his own lands, but Robin is made in the same heroic mold: an outcast who manages events as they develop, his superiority over those who have exiled him wonderfully apparent. Together the two define a more effective hero, a figure who concentrates on reestablishing the nation and instilling harmony in its people.

This recovery takes its most dramatic form with Ivanhoe's victories over the Norman faction. Ivanhoe demonstrates complete superiority as the Disinherited Knight neutralizing the Normans' perverse power, thus signalling a reversal in the ill effects of their tyranny. In a key scene, Ivanhoe unhorses Bois-Guilbert, who in extricating himself "from [his] stirrups and fallen steed was . . . stung with madness" (98–99). Ivanhoe displays his skill in manipulating the "icon of power" (the horse) to his own advantage, depriving his enemy from moving forward or backward, immobilizing him. Equestrian iconography describes Bois-Guilbert's final humiliation on the second day of the tournament: "the Templar's horse had bled much, and gave way under the shock of the Disinherited Knight's charge." As he attempts to escape Ivanhoe, Bois-Guilbert falls victim to the animal's collapse, and he "roll[s] on the field, encumbered with the stirrup, from which he was unable to draw his foot" (141).

Ivanhoe's achievements serve as a mirror to Locksley's trial by archery that duplicates the formalistic patterns of the tournament. When Robin defeats the Norman archer Hubert, the tournament in any meaningful sense is over. The overwhelming victory is not merely of Saxon over Norman but of natural goodness and social responsibility over madness and absurdity.

Another important, but lesser, series of trials also concludes in this section, and that is the contrasting scenes of feasting. From Cedric's hall of oaks to Prince John's "higharch'd hall" of Castle Ashby, food and feasting become secondary indicators of cultural values. Scott uses food allusions much in the same way as Chaucer, who in *The Canterbury Tales* refers often to the food habits of each pilgrim.

Both writers suggested people were what they ate; the kind, preparation, and amount of food explain social class and moral condition.

Prince John's banquet, in its display of elaborate ceremony and table splendor, is reminiscent of the astonishing artifice at the Ashby-de-la-Zouche tournament. Guests are seated at tables groaning under the weight of foods prepared so exotically that they are shocked by such luxury. Imported delicacies are surrounded by quantities of "rich pastry, . . . simnel bread and wastel cakes" (157). Wastel and simnel breads made of the finest white flour and baked to the consistency of a modern French croissant were often known as "Lord's bread" or "noble bread." The lavish table symbolizes Prince John's manipulation of the power, dependence, and mutual obligation bonding the host to his dependents. Feasts were certainly conceived as the epitome of love and fellowship, but the opportunities for abusing this ideal were well known even in Scott's time.

In his portrayal of tournament chivalry, Scott parallels its absurdities with the Norman's feast ethic; their abdication of the traditional virtues of hospitality embraces instead the immorality of luxury. For example, serving Athelstane, the unready gourmet, an exotic "karum pie," a pastry dish containing small birds whose meat was cunningly sweetened by a diet of grapes, points up a new series of contrasts between the two cultures. The Normans assert their social rank and power over the Saxons in a kind of banquet hall warfare. Each dish and the accompanying rich wines demonstrate a contempt for the simple, rural Saxon palate. Athelstane and Cedric as proud representatives of an ancient order are confounded and angered in this debased society. Athelstane can only manage a timid gastronomic criticism amidst this groundswell of luxury: "that he would fight a dozen men" if he could leave a place "where they put so much garlic into their pottage" (224).

The Normans use of elegant artifice changes the essential nature of the raw ingredients: the natural becomes through a kind of alchemy something artificial. The comparisons readers can draw between Norman cuisine and the food habits of Chaucer's Pardoner and Summoner are no accident. When the Pardoner condemns (hypocritically) "these cooks, how they must grind and pound and strain / And transform substance into accident" (11.538-39).[21] He makes quite correctly a philosophical distinction between "substance," the real nature of a thing, and "accident," its merely sensory qualities, such as flavor. Clearly, Norman luxury interferes with the well-grounded Saxon order of things. But we, as readers, are aware that the order of things Cedric cherished has in fact been much eroded, and the Saxons must come to terms with the changing cultural pressures. Yet there is every reason to note the loss incurred as the two cultures clash. Corruption, rebellion, and political chaos have upset the individual's moral equilibrium. The feast has become an exercise in gluttony, where both excessive eating and excessive drinking lead to a loss of self-control.

The Saxons hold an entirely different view of food and feasting, emphasizing temperance and moderation. The farm dinner given to the Prior and Templar at Rotherwood serves as a model of discriminating taste and healthy moderation. Cedric sets the tone of the feast with a warning against "pride of table," while implying that gluttony corrupts the rich. "Your homely fare is before you, feed, and let welcome make amends for hard fare" (44). No luxury here, no imported, exotic foodstuffs, no elegant artifice masking substance—Cedric is against culinary extravagance. All the dishes reflect the immediate results of domestic hunters and gatherers who provide "fowls, deer, goats, and hares, the various kinds of fish . . . fruits and honey" (44). The Saxon lives on the local economy, cherishes its inherent power, the strength and richness of the land. Cedric's identification with the land, his actual and symbolic connection to the green world of the forest, remains his true source of wealth.

The same moderation exhibited in the Saxon feast becomes a metaphor for Saxon virtues in general. Cedric and Athelstane, while imprisoned at Torquilstone, discuss the destruction of prudence, regulation, and restraint in culinary terms. In each segment, Cedric reviews English history before and after the Norman invasion, punctuated only by Athelstane's frequent requests for food from his Norman captors. The scene and the symbolic aspects of food are highly suggestive of the two cultures' relative strengths. "It cannot be their [the Normans'] purpose to starve us outright . . . I see no preparations for serving dinner" (221). Athelstane's desperation implies his willingness to eat Norman food and give up any hope of eating Saxon fare. Cedric warns against this defeatist attitude in the strongest terms: "Far better was our homely diet, eaten in peace and liberty, than the luxurious dainties, the love of which that delivered us as bound men to the foreign conqueror!" (222).

Cedric believes the Saxon defeat was a failure of moral virtue, a sinking down in the mire of luxury. Athelstane's acceptance of the status quo and obvious annoyance with Cedric's interpretations of history turn into an opportunity of using Cedric's own words and ideas against him. In mocking tones, the younger man finds it remarkable that Cedric can remember ancient history but forget "the very hours of dinner"; "I should hold very humble diet a luxury at present" (222). For the first time in the novel, Cedric acknowledges the inevitable defeat of the Saxon cause, a realization that marks his voice, posture, and gestures with failure and frustration. The worst of his fears he keeps at bay with bold expressions of belief in the tide-turning powers of Athelstane and the arranged marriage of Athelstane and Rowena; but they must now coexist with his new perspective on this last, best hope of Saxon kingship. "It is time lost," Cedric remarks while studying Athelstane, "to speak to him of aught else but that which concerns his appetite! . . . Alas that so dull a spirit should be lodged in so goodly a form" (222).

The issue of Athelstane's hunger sets off a journey from physical to mental to emotional dependency that epitomizes his weakness, especially suggestive in the "appearance" reference. He becomes associated with apparelled or adorned food decorated to create an appearance or an illusion. Cedric has pretended that Athelstane was something other than what he is. Athelstane might have turned his hunger into energy to fight for what his people want; instead of understanding its liberating potential, however, he allows his dependency to become obsession. The misuse of food and the ceremony of eating further degrade the Saxon cause, symbolically confirming its domination.

CONCLUSION

Scott is careful to sort out for the reader an important distinction regarding his romance form. From the earliest appearance of Ivanhoe to his wounding in the lists at Ashby, we have been uncomfortably aware that he lacks the superhuman qualities of the typical romantic hero. Even at the moment of his tournament victory, the handsome Ivanhoe can only display a "countenance . . . as pale as death, and marked with blood," before losing consciousness (144). Robin of Locksley appears "a stout well-set yeoman, arrayed in Lincoln green," capable of securing not only the approval of the common people but also the respect of the nobility. Robin succeeds in cutting across the bounds of romantic fiction; his character is improved by human virtues and lent verisimilitude by the reality of the green world of Sherwood Forest. What Ivanhoe lacks because he is too closely bound to what he calls the "pure light of chivalry" has been balanced through the effort of Robin.

Scott has argued for a more realistic view of the ethos of chivalry by, in Kenneth Sroka's description, "mirroring the historical truth about the institution of chivalry."22 The tournament at Ashby, the Norman knights, and Ivanhoe himself as well as Richard all reflect chivalry's decline. The corruption of the chivalric ideal—the conversion of love into lust, freedom into tyranny, and courage into cowardice—Scott explains "by portraying the worst abuses of chivalry in its villains and by humanizing its perfect heroes" (Sroka, 653). Yet for all of Robin's moral and physical virtues, he still does not supplant Ivanhoe. Though Robin represents the best interests of the country and people for whom Ivanhoe is the moral and spiritual envoy, Ivanhoe is the true agent of his king.

With remarkable cleverness Scott has managed to keep his hero nameless for 12 chapters, and now at a dramatic moment, under the Iliad motto "Heroes approach . . . stand forth," he does so. "The name of Ivanhoe was no sooner pronounced than it flew from mouth to mouth with . . . eagerness" (145). Though we have considered why his identity is hidden for so long, the choice of his hero's name remains a curiosity in itself, one the author does little to clarify. Scott suggests in his 1830 introduction to the text that the word came to him in an old rhyme (conveniently, the title is forgotten) whose historical connections he remembers. The name refers to one of three estates (the others: Tring and Wing) forfeited by "the celebrated Hampden" during a heated tennis match with of all people, Edward, The Black Prince, the fourteenth century's greatest soldier. Scott slyly suggests his attraction to the name was in its neutrality; no connections except "the sound" of England could be made with the novel's content. A closer analysis of English personal nomenclature implies, however, some possibilities that show Scott intended quite the opposite of a name "empty of associations."

The English Christian name *Ivo* derives from both the Old French *Ivon* and the Old German *Iv*. With the latter, *Iv* refers to the yew, an evergreen tree with hard, fine-grained wood. The later associations with English oak in the forest, in Cedric's home, and, most significantly, in the uprooted oak on Ivanhoe's shield consolidate the earliest images of the land, those intimated in the novel's primary figure. Scott effectively translates the *Ivo,* a name brought to England shortly after the Norman Conquest and a favorite with Anglo-Normans, as the name of a disputed estate. Since Wilfred was disinherited by his father, King Richard grants the former Saxon estate, Ivanhoe, to this landless man, a figure caught between two cultures without the defining element of property.

A recent critic notes the significance of the Ivanhoe estate becoming the representative estate ruled by a figure who allies the Norman and Saxon cultures.23 The "symmetry of this closure" seems richer when one translates his Christian name, Wilfred. As a compound of the Old English *will* (will) and *frith* (peace), Scott recalls St. Wilfrith or Wilfrid (c. 634–709), Bishop of York and a remarkable figure, who has over 50 churches dedicated to him. The appropriateness of Wilfred's name engages the reader, since the hero wills peace into being and unites disparate cultures into one kingdom. To understand the function of the hero's names is to see how property empowers symbolic form, including forms of identity, and how symbols participate in the dynamics of property, including the dynamics of inheritance and disinheritance.

Ivanhoe's early actions end with his wounding; he is now forced into a passive role in which his education, his sense of himself and of humanity in general, must be reevaluated. He must come to terms with his romantic ideals, understand them in relation to the realities of a divided England.

Scott plays on these issues in the highly suggestive chapter 16, where Richard, disguised as The Black Sluggard (Le Noir Faineant), discovers the hermitage of the Clerk of Copmanhurst and spends the evening in a curious interview that metaphorically delineates the critical dilemma. "'The road—the road!' vociferated the knight; 'give me directions for the road'" (175). Here even the King asks for guidance, and in his own land too; he receives an answer he cannot understand and questions how the Clerk can survive in such unpromising surroundings. "The good keeper of the forest," said the hermit, "hath allowed me the use of these animals to protect my solitude until the time shall mend" (176).

As Ivanhoe must accept the status of observer and student, Richard must also agree that he is lost and in need of further knowledge and education. As he explores the mysteries of the forest—"a broken path—a precipice—a ford—and a morass" (175), Richard also explores the limits of his inner landscape. He will, as has Ivanhoe, reconcile the importance of humanity and the ease with which people are willing to compromise their humanity in the implacable pursuit of their self-interest with his own need for adventure and extravagance.

As we see in the next chapter of this study, the landscape of the novel is fashioned by the continued struggle against recklessness and fanaticism. The bonding of Richard and Locksley as they struggle to free the imprisoned party, including Ivanhoe, now under the tutelage of Rebecca, culminates in the next important stage of the novel, the scene at Torquilstone.

6

Torquilstone: Chaos Articulated

"The daylight had dawned upon the glades of the oak forest. The green boughs glittered with all their pearls of dew. The hind led her fawn from the covert of high fern . . . and no huntsman was there to watch or interrupt the stately hart, as he paced at the head of the antlered herd" (347). The serenity and beauty of this scene concluding the central third of the novel has been achieved only at the greatest cost to the human society that it symbolically represents. Scott captures here all the richness and promise of the novel's thematic interest in the events that frame the siege itself. With civil disorder and corruption rampant throughout the countryside, and with the ineffectual John consistently adding to the disintegration, the issues of national identity and social leadership become paramount. For Scott, nothing will serve but a national purification, a cleansing in which hypocrisy and truth are revealed clearly in the actions of the characters. The major Norman and Saxon figures here undergo a far more exacting crisis than at Ashby and are transformed by it. Scott manages their personal relationships so that the reader can appreciate their quite human suffering, while recognizing, too, the evolving political and social world of which they are a part, and which informs his theme of social progress.

Forest Magic

The Torquilstone section opens with one of the novel's most important unifying metaphors—landscape as the vehicle for mystery, magic, and a kind of hypnotic power. Scott's technique of charging the forest with a real vitality recalls Kurt Wittig's comment: "Scott . . . endowed landscape with a life of its own, to the extent of making it one of the protagonists in his novels."[24] After the surprising events at Ashby, Cedric and his party start home only to meet Isaac and Rebecca with a horse-drawn litter. With a few well chosen words, Rebecca convinces Rowena to persuade Cedric to offer the protection of the group to the Jews. Impending evil is suggested by the description of the wood, since the group must "plunge into its recesses" populated by "outlaws whom oppression and poverty had driven to despair" (199). Landscape is more than simply a background: it is itself teeming with life, and everything living must fight for survival.

Ironically, Robin of Locksley and his band of outlaws seem the only group to be truly one with the environment; as in Emily Brontë and Thomas Hardy, the land tolerates intruders but is hardly changed by their intrusion. The forest, for Scott, provides elaborate word pictures, offering "paths to yet wilder scenes of sylvan solitude" (10), encouraging us to examine more closely the chaos of this world. Society's exiles, an Ivanhoe and Locksley, understand the mystery of the forest, and the Norman aristocracy and Prince John are the true villains; they attempt to use its "broken and discolored light" to their own advantage. In their assumed role as Saxon outlaws, De Bracy and the Templar attack the travelers, taking them all prisoners; they violate, in essence, the sanctity of the forest. No matter that outlaws are known to prey on travelers, such Saxon "banditti were generally supposed to respect the persons and property of their countrymen" (199).

This Norman group's violation of the land—its values—has everything to do with Scott's rendering here of an embryonic national identity. The arrival in the forest of these self-interested foreigners who represent corrupted chivalric and Christian ideals precipitates the reappearance of Richard, who is occupied in educating himself as to the virtues and vices of his people. While enjoying Friar Tuck's jovial company, Richard pauses and becomes quite serious; he recognizes the value of the priest's insight into human behavior: "it is true that all have their enemies; and there be those in this land whom I would rather speak to through the bars of my helmet than barefaced" (209).

From the earliest moment when John and his faction had heard of Richard's arrival in England, they had begun to crumble as a cohesive party. They lacked reverence for their monarch, dishonored the conventions of the *comitatus* (the companions of the King), and refused to sacrifice themselves for their betters. Yet the forest outlaws—Robin and his Merrymen—display the exact opposite behavior; their response to the unknown knight is to acknowledge his humanity by naming him. The insightful Locksley identifies the knight by his past actions; "you are he who decided the victory to the advantage of the English . . . at Ashby" (212). Richard answers with the chivalric imperative of fairness and honor as the code demanded, but his words seem hollow. Locksley, who has registered the triumph of experience over theory, neatly casts aside the "duty of a true knight" even as an issue. His requirements are plain and unsentimental: "For my purpose thou shouldst be as well a good Englishman as a good knight; for that which I have to speak of concerns, indeed, the duty of every honest man" (212).

Again Richard listens without fully comprehending, but he agrees to join Locksley to attack Torquilstone in the hope of freeing Cedric and his party—doing so because of his knightly vows. Emphasizing that every man, whether knight or king or commoner, is an integral part of the community, Locksley repeats the principles of his code: "I am a friend of my country, and of my country's friends" (212–13). Torquilstone, it would seem, takes on greater significance than as a place of imprisonment (and death) for the corrupt and selfish; for the sensible man who exchanges his right to selfish action for the protection of society, Torquilstone is a place of rebirth and reintegration. Richard, who finally grasps the difference in the yeoman's character, replies, "I have been accustomed to study men's countenances, and I can read in thine honesty and resolution" (213).

It would appear Richard has set aside the stylized idiom of chivalry for plain speaking, thus suggesting that he recognizes the gulf separating aristocratic and middle-class cultures. Admittedly, he possesses a charismatic power capable of enchanting all who surround him; though a reckless crusader and an unstable king, Richard embodies both England's disordered past and its precarious present. Robin, as *Ivanhoe* has earlier done, must cleave to him as a disciple to his master. If England is to achieve greatness, Scott here implies, it must have kings who encourage national unity. By agreeing to join and then lead Robin's band of outlaws against the Norman leaders, Richard initiates the return of law and order. Clearly, he has moved beyond his earlier role of reticent Black Sluggard, rescuing *Ivanhoe* but then disappearing only to reappear as Friar Tuck's drinking companion. When Richard agrees with Robin's analysis that England needs good men who love their country, he is acting not only as his country's providential protector, but also as a man who can learn and progress.

Scott encourages such thinking by bringing the man to the moment: *Ivanhoe* lies wounded and inactive; Robin, though brave and resourceful, is bound by his class and culture to respect the knight; and Richard emerges as the moral focus. Even the Templar, as he surveys the enemy's approach, notices the change. "These men approach with more touch of discipline than could have been judged, however, they come by it" (292), he concludes. Blinded by the fanaticism of their pride, these Norman knights cannot recognize the alliance of humane law and natural goodness that will destroy them, and thus restore England to its former health.

"Fiends of Hell"

The struggle between the Saxons and the Normans degenerates into the worst forms of brutality and ghoulish excess when the conflict moves from the natural world of Sherwood Forest to the dark, manufactured recesses of the Norman castles. Torquilstone, Reginald Front-de-Boeuf's fortress, receives Maurice De Bracy's kidnapped victims as prisoners.

As if to underscore their divisive rigidity, Scott separates the Saxon prisoners. Cedric and Athelstane go to a large room "rising on clumsy Saxon pillars," formerly the great hall of the castle, but "now abandoned to meaner purposes" (219). Rowena, isolated from her protector Cedric as well as her servant Elgitha, must resort to her own strength of character while imprisoned in an apartment "fitted up with some crude attempts at ornament and magnificence" but now in a state of decay and neglect, "judged most fitting for the accommodation of the Saxon heiress" (235). Isaac of York is immediately taken to the castle's torture chamber, where the fanatic Front-de-Boeuf indicts him as "the most accursed dog of an accursed race" (228). His daughter, Rebecca, is segregated "in a distant and sequestered turret" (244), where she encounters the Saxon aboriginal Ulrica, who has never before spoken of Front-de-Boeuf's many crimes, including parricide and sexual assault. Now, in the presence of the solicitous Rebecca, the old Saxon crone reveals all the outrageous Norman vices, concluding "there was not a room, not a step of the stair, that was not slippery with their [her family's] blood" (245).

Scott plays the green world of Sherwood Forest, with its potential for growth and change, against the unhealthy, contrived horrors of the castle. Informing this section are the ghastly paraphernalia of ruined Gothic castles and the sensationalist language typical of the romances of Ann Radcliffe and Matthew Lewis. Drawing on his knowledge of *The Mysteries of Udolpho* and *The Monk*, as well as Lewis's play, *The Castle Spectre* (1797), and the medievalism of Macpherson and Chatterton, Scott arranges, as Francis Hart reminds us, "a chaos articulated with striking formal precision" (Hart 1966, 161). This clarity Scott brought to the themes and descriptions of terror-romanticism further suggests his skill in moving beyond the earliest Gothic theatrics of Walpole's *Castle of Otranto*. Certainly the general flavor of *Otranto* is present, but Scott's passion for historical detail reduces these fancies into a species closer to the truth. The key difference becomes one of sounding the depths behind the images of the haunted castle and reaching what Eino Railo calls "natural nature."[25]

The Normans who function as perverse jailers move in and about the castle, torturing their prisoners mentally, accusing them of everything from murder to wrongful kinds of love. Scott punctuates each crisis with the insistent notes of the attackers' hunting horn, thus heightening the suspense, while turning our attention toward the inevitable battle. When Richard and Locksley finally attack, the disorder begs for redress of the public peace and a return to civilization.

At the beginning of these scenes De Bracy arrives at Torquilstone with prisoners in tow. Sounding his horn three times, he, along with Bois-Guilbert, demands recognition from the castle guards and seeks a reconciliation with their faction. Instead of a symbolic rejoining of the three Norman knights, however, there is discord; they share little unity of purpose. Typically, their plans for successfully bringing off this outrageous kidnapping are narrow and unimaginative. Yet their confusion neatly balances the comic absurdity of the Saxons, Cedric and Athelstane. Cedric, as we have seen, lacks originality and breadth of mind, desirous as he is of keeping his authority and privilege, though unwilling to use his common sense to accept change. Rather, he disowns his son, who has disobeyed him and, more to the point, has "relinquish[ed] the manners and customs of his fathers" (159). With his new "son," Athelstane, Cedric must come to terms with his rejection of *Ivanhoe* and with his own divisive rigidity. "'Alas!' said he, looking at Athelstane with compassion, 'that so dull a spirit should be lodged in so goodly a form! Alas that such an enterprise as the regeneration of England should turn on a hinge so imperfect!'" (222). Unable to ignore Athelstane's perpetual irresponsibility, Cedric has begun the process, unconsciously at first, of comparing his two "sons."

Ivanhoe, who has proven his readiness, has won new recognition in the old Saxon's eyes, and Athelstane, whose animal nature controls his every motion, has shown once again a ridiculous mania for food and drink. The first scene of prisoner visitations ends with Athelstane's silly challenge to fight Front-de-Boeuf, offered while nearly choking on a large mouthful of food. At this precise moment of pure bathos, the rescuer's horn sounds outside the castle, signalling an end to the farce and the beginning of a more frightening scene.

MY DUCATS AND MY DAUGHTER

Isaac of York is dragged to a dungeon-vault of the castle and asked to choose between torture by fire or payment of 1000 pounds of silver to

Front-de-Boeuf. The Jew demands the release of his daughter, Rebecca, only to discover she has been given to the Templar. From the chapter's opening epigraph, Scott suggests a view of Isaac that recalls Shakespeare's Shylock: "My daughter! O my ducats! O my daughter!" The ducats-daughter juxtaposition makes Shylock ridiculous and thus an appropriate object for mockery; Shakespeare gives full expression to the common Elizabethan prejudice that a Jew is only really concerned about money. Scott proceeds in much the same fashion, but typically reverses the stereotype, creating in Isaac a more consistent, more integrated character. Though he never defends Isaac's usury, Scott is more willing to condemn Norman greed as at least equally to blame for this state of corruption.

The stress on human compassion becomes obvious when Isaac pleads with Front-de-Boeuf: "It is impossible that your purpose can be real! The good God of nature never made a heart capable of exercising such cruelty!" (229). If it is true that Isaac is really thinking of his money, it is also true that the Jew appeals to the Norman's Christian compassion. Front-de-Boeuf hears the appeal for mercy and rejects it. "Dost thou think that I, who have seen a town sacked, in which thousands of my Christian countrymen perished by sword . . . will blench from my purpose for . . . one single wretched Jew?" (229). If Scott suggests Isaac's motivating principle is that "it's no sin to deceive a Christian," he balances such a feeling against the most cynical (if not callous) attitudes of Christians toward their fellow human beings.

The promotion of vice anywhere in society, Scott believes, encourages its growth throughout the culture. The Norman perversion of power cries out for a rebellion, an uprising that not even Isaac, blunted by years of persecution, can ignore. Front-de-Boeuf imprisons him and threatens torture while extorting money, thus evoking sympathy for the man and his defiance. Ironically, Isaac's revolt, when it comes following the news of Rebecca's threatened seduction, prepares the way for the Saxon attack on the castle. The refusal to validate the status quo, brought on by severe emotional anxiety in the victims, results in a violent, physical response. Scott manipulates the passions of both victims and jailers, thus heightening the dramatic effect. The revolution has come about because of the use and abuse of power by a member of the governing class. Clearly, and quite memorably here, Isaac cannot turn to the law because his oppressor *is* the law. "I will pay thee nothing . . . unless my daughter is delivered to me in safety and honor" (234).

Isaac becomes symbolically identified with the disinherited *Ivanhoe* and champions Rebecca's life over his own, acting with courage, nobility, and humanity. Deepening his narrative by first displacing romance with realism, Scott now reverts to the romance formula at just the critical moment when torture seems unavoidable. A blast of a bugle further disturbs the Gothic scene, and the reader turns to a more serene, yet no less ominous, meeting with Rowena and De Bracy.

"The Jargon of Troubadour"

Aristocratic women of the twelfth century were subjected to increased restrictions in virtually every sphere of their lives. With the proliferation of new, centralized institutions in church and state, women found themselves more and more circumscribed economically, politically, and socially. Great families often excluded women from inheritance to preserve the power and influence of the patriarchy. Rowena's present circumstance is a result of her guardian Cedric's wish that she marry Athelstane, last of the royal Saxons, and reject *Ivanhoe*, who set aside his father's hatred of the Normans.

According to Cedric's standard, Rowena must accept the responsibility for rebuilding the Saxon order; she must spurn any suggestion of a reconciliation with the Normans. Her integrity as an independent woman is restricted, as Cedric's right to arrange her marriage is encouraged, by custom. Only when Athelstane recognizes his inability to take *Ivanhoe*'s place does he petition Cedric for Rowena's release. Later, Rebecca, as she leaves England, sanctifies the impending marriage of *Ivanhoe* and Rowena: "Yet keep [the jewels] lady . . . you have power, rank, command, influence; we have wealth" (517–18). Since Rowena has no economic power, she cannot present her husband with a dowry; ironically, it is Rebecca who provides Rowena the money that, given her family connections, will allow her to make a vital contribution to the advancement of her new family.

Scott's interest in Rowena has been characterized as severely limited; she exists to give the hero someone to marry, she is as insipid as most of Scott's historical heroines. Without arguing here against this general disparagement of Scott's heroines, one might nonetheless recall the powers of Diana Vernon in *Rob Roy*, Jeanie Deans in *The Heart of Midlothian*, and, of course, Rebecca. No doubt, Rowena cannot measure up to the dramatic strength of these women, but she does engage us; she has an active mind and a pleasing vitality. Her appearance in the Ashby section, Scott there introducing her and then making plain *Ivanhoe*'s unswerving fidelity to her by naming her the Queen of Beauty and Love, suggests her power. Cedric, for all his dominance as Rowena's guardian, cannot dazzle her even "with the prospect of a visionary throne"; more to the point, Rowena considers Cedric's plea for Saxon independence neither "practicable nor desirable" (197).

After Rowena's capture by the Normans in Sherwood Forest and her imprisonment at Torquilstone, she manages, in an early interview with her captor Maurice De Bracy, to expose one of the major themes of the novel: the brutal reality of chivalry. Scott develops carefully in a kind of three-part structure his assessment of chivalry's romantic extravagances. Rowena's unchivalric treatment at the hands of De Bracy begs comparison with the horrific narrative of the Saxon woman Ulrica, who is assaulted by Sir Reginald Front-de-Boeuf after he kills her family, then keeps her as his mistress before finally throwing her aside. Scott concludes this portrait of chivalry's deterioration with Rebecca's courageous response to Bois-Guilbert, and then the famous debate with the wounded *Ivanhoe*.

Though Rowena's behavior during the Torquilstone captivity has often been unfavorably compared with Rebecca's magnificent conduct, the pressures she suffers are quite different from Rebecca's, and her response appropriate. De Bracy's brand of chivalry reveals a selfishness that may well be allegorical of the savage passions so theatrically on display at Torquilstone. Here good and evil are in stark contrast, and each level of the castle reveals a variation on the perverse. From Isaac's suffering in the dungeon, at the sound of the trumpet we move up the castle steps to Rowena's chamber, and then to Rebecca's cell, where the contrasts between the two women are drawn more sharply. Finally, on the parapet, the suffering Ulrica signals an end to her torture by vowing revenge.

Scott's real achievement here, fully realized only in Rebecca, rests on his brilliant portrayals of the mind under duress, calling forth its deepest fears and primitive superstitions, and connecting the reader with these in a remarkably effective way. Rowena opposes De Bracy's words with a thoughtfully conceived attack on his use of language. Arguing first that his language is decadent and outmoded, she insists on the pragmatic and explicit when communicating ideas. Foreshadowing the later Rebecca-Ivanhoe debate on chivalry, Rowena finds that De Bracy's "troubadour jargon forms no apology for the violence of robber," suggesting that his own actions have corrupted his chivalrous language. De Bracy becomes "confused" and "speak[s] in a tone more natural to him than that of the effected gallantry which he had at first adopted" (237). Rowena sharpens the discussion, demanding an end to "courtly language," and, in effect, humanizes him.

There is little point in speculating how far Scott might have taken his novel had he more fully imitated the eighteenth-century novelist Samuel Richardson, an obvious influence here in the Rowena-Rebecca chapters. The epistolary technique is brought to remarkable fruition in Richardson's *Pamela* (1740) and *Clarissa* (1747–48); had Scott used it here, Rowena would have had an opportunity to explain more fully her later comments to De Bracy. Rowena's Pamela-like trial, in which she shows superior strength over De Bracy (he resembles Richardson's Mr. B., both corrupted and corrupting) accords her a kind of recognition she has long sought but always been denied. Insisting on the integrity of her moral virtue, Rowena, in effect, cleanses Torquilstone: "courtesy of tongue" cannot "veil churlishness of deed," she well notes, and "thy language . . . cannot be reconciled with the horrors it seems to express" (237, 239).

De Bracy, now properly chastened for straying from what is easy, natural, and unaffected, replies in new, "bold" language, but his words still lack moral resonance. Scott cannot here afford to prolong the episode; to engage De Bracy or any of the Norman knights in a long exercise of moral reformation would detract from Rebecca, his hero-ine. He can, however, declare the necessity for such reform and point the finger. Ultimately, under the brutal pressures of De Bracy's bold-ness, Rowena breaks down and cries great sentimental tears for Ivanhoe's desperate fate. The elaborate pantomime ends with the author's intrusion as he seeks to move us (not surprisingly) to Rebecca's quarters.

Do we now know more about the private motives behind Rowena's love for *Ivanhoe*? Has Scott explored her psyche? He has not carefully delineated thoughts and feelings, but created instead a memorable scene where fear, love, compassion, and hate rise sponta-neously. Rowena reflects the mores of Scott's society: for a woman, the measure of success is a good marriage. Her innocence and good-ness, as well as determination, will bring about this happy result.

DESCENT TO A LOWER WORLD

The terrible acts committed at Front-de-Boeuf's castle begin in the actual depths of its dungeons with Isaac's torture. As Scott builds to the great battle, the Saxons in triumph wresting the fortress away from the Normans, he emphasizes here the climactic moment symbol-ic of the descent into this lower world. Though it is in fact on a floor above the torture chambers, Rebecca's prison room, where she must undergo Brian Bois-Guilbert's interview, suggests the confusion and corruption of the world into which she has fallen, her innocence now threatened, her freedom lost.

What makes the greatest emotional impression on us is Rebecca's endurance, her suffering and patience, in the face of Brian's threats. Though obviously physically weaker, she is still strong emotionally—spiritually. She has earlier taken a great risk in rescuing Ivanhoe from Norman hands, and now she willingly offers to die for her principles. Her sacrifice would prolong the lives of Isaac and Ivanhoe, and Rebecca freely accepts the hazards of descending to this lower, vicious world. This offer is rejected twice, first when the soul-dead Ulrica (appropriately willing to die like her family) prepares her revenge against the Normans, and later when the fatalistic Bois-Guilbert backs off from his threatened rape and begs Rebecca not to throw herself from the castle: "let there be peace between us" (253). In essence, Rebecca's offer redeems lesser mortals like Isaac and Ivanhoe and permits an ascent to a higher world, outside the castle, for Rebecca and for those she helps.

In thus representing her, Scott heightens Rebecca's humanizing effect; she becomes a classic example of the romantic virgin, imbued with life-giving powers. Not only has she saved Ivanhoe from dying as a result of his Ashby wound, but Rebecca indirectly employs her remarkable powers of healing upon Bois-Guilbert. In effect, her effort redeems what little humanity may remain in the man: he falls more deeply in love with her and discovers chivalric traits within himself long buried. Her integrity shames him into recalling something of his better nature: "I am not naturally that which you have seen me—hard, selfish and relentless" (253).

As significant as this display of courage and goodness is in revealing Rebecca's character, she also possesses a high degree of intelligence and an astuteness for management. This makes her more complex, of course, and more attractive. She seems less inhibited, more active and assertive. Scott suggests her real value is as a thinking person; she uses her intellectual and spiritual powers to get the better of blundering chauvinists like Bois-Guilbert, as well as to instruct the disoriented (wounded) Ivanhoe. Bois-Guilbert takes his first step toward self-awareness when he recounts the last time he felt and acted as a human being instead of as an automaton: "Truly did I love her [his Norman fiancée], and bitterly did I revenge me of her broken faith. . . . Since that day I have separated myself from life and its ties" (254).

Shocked at the cost to him of such a stand, Rebecca demands to know what could be gained by "such an absolute sacrifice." Scott reveals the selfishness of a man who seeks vengeance and "the prospects of ambition." Rebecca, though quite horrified at Bois-Guilbert's weakness and utter hypocrisy, even in the face of vows he has sworn to uphold, does not berate him; instead she simply asserts the principal ethic of her philosophy: "[never] surrender . . . the rights which are dearest to humanity" (254). Bois-Guilbert blusters a few short sentences more, and only the sound of the bugle saves him from admitting the complete absurdity of his position.

A woman who is self-aware, who despite the bigotry of her society has a sense of an autonomous self, and who acts in accordance with her own self-image could exert the force necessary to undermine villainy and shore up goodness. Rebecca's liberation originates in her own suffering and in her recognition that the values of the male-dominated society are ludicrously inferior; yet her anger does not close off her dialogue with men. Since her self-awareness derives not only from her suffering but also from her understanding of men's loss, beginning with that of her father, Bois-Guilbert, and *Ivanhoe*, she knows her liberation of spirit must represent a freedom for men too, both overcoming their imposed roles. The imminent battle seems a most effective vehicle for the social action needed to overcome the laws under which the corrupt men in power have prospered at the expense of women and nature.

THE MASK OF CHIVALRY

Four blasts of the attacker's bugle have at last brought the Norman knights together, forcing them into a mutual association against destruction. Yet their destruction is assured; the theme of social progress, clear from the beginning, remains unassailable now—all must be changed in what is nothing less than a representative national purification. This cleansing of the national consciousness requires a reconciliation of the two dominant powers, Saxon and Norman, under one leader who possesses both legitimate political authority and a natural humanity.

King Richard's management of this political situation, like his command of strategy and his intelligence and diplomacy, undergird the battle scenes. But Scott renders these scenes in an unexpected fashion. Instead of using direct intervention by the narrator in the action and dialogue sequence, he employs dual observers, one inquiring and searching for peace and the other relentlessly seeking vengeance. These women narrators, each of whom cares for a wounded man, describe the ensuing battle in terms particular to their own point of view.

It is worth recalling the many tensions, literary as well as organic, that inform this section of the novel. Scott had been much influenced by Cervantes's *Don Quixote;* he was taken by how the Knight of La Mancha's actions as a "redresser of wrongs" may have been ridiculous for the time, even though the values he espoused were virtuous. Like Scott himself, Cervantes subjected chivalry to an intense (if comic) scrutiny. Both were profoundly interested in how the decadent stylizations of this outmoded ethos could nonetheless sometimes prove capable of supporting real feeling. Like the Don, whose antics and self-delusions may make him appear silly, yet whose moral probity we never question, such characters as Rebecca and Ulrica here evoke just these same concerns. The values of chivalry that frame (and, arguably, define) these battle scenes are worthy.

Contemporary histories reveal the tensions implicit in chivalric life of the late Middle Ages; Scott was concerned with the use of the term *chivalry*. For Scott, the chivalric ethos in *Ivanhoe* is a code for discussing human behavior in any age. He would ask implicitly time and again how it is possible for chivalry to ennoble savagery in the name of glory and yet sustain heroism and moral courage so impressive that generations would be inspired by such exemplary men. These ambivalences do not weaken his description here of the battle, or more particularly the inset narratives of Rebecca and *Ivanhoe* and Ulrica. Instead, they suggest quite effectively the irrationalities at play, as well as the manner in which they might temper his visionary ideal of a new England. Scott has not lost sight of himself, nor his themes in some pointless fancy; but if his historiography seems useful, it is because the vision has been sharpened against the conflicting drama of both past and present.

Rebecca's first important speech to the injured *Ivanhoe* appears as a flashback at the moment she and Isaac secreted *Ivanhoe* away from Ashby. Here, on the road to York (Scott cleverly positions this interchange immediately before the Saxon assault), Rebecca announces why the later battle must be fought. "Thou hast been restored to thy country when it most needed the assistance of a strong hand and a true heart, . . . be of good courage, and trust that thou art preserved for some marvel which thine arm shall work before this people" (304). With intelligence and insight, she realizes *Ivanhoe* represents a historical force, far more significant than his individual concerns. *Ivanhoe* embodies a transition from one stage of history to another. By placing him on neutral ground Scott can then portray the opposing social forces as they interact with one another.

Rebecca's role as narrator of the great battle provides a countervailing psychology and historical perspective, whereas *Ivanhoe* must always reply with the expected noble sentiment. Whatever may have been chivalry's inherent vices and defects, it seems indisputable that Scott intends to complicate the notion of war; as Francis Bacon states, war becomes "the highest trial of right when princes and states . . . shall put themselves upon the justice of God for the deciding of their controversies."[26] Rebecca's effort toward peace and reconciliation ironically becomes a powerful weapon against war, especially war validated by the duties and courtesies of chivalry.

Ivanhoe's reference to the battle as a "brave game" men play at is given satiric import by Scott's metaphor linking it to the storm—"what we have heard was but the distant mutterings of the storm: it will burst . . . in all its fury" (310); nature is here a corroborative force. Chivalry turns into sport when grown men can—when it suits them—display fellowship, discipline, and physical prowess, while all the time doing something morally indefensible. *Ivanhoe*, who must depend on Rebecca's view of things, feels a desperation much like his twentieth-century descendants who were urged forward in World War I by the well-known verse: "Up, Up, Up and up / Face your game and play it."[27] Nature's coercion in the process only heightens the need to summon valor at all costs: the imputation of cowardice is the most damaging charge that can be brought against a knight. Going to war is a matter of honor. *Ivanhoe* accepts this, as do all who live according to the chivalrous code; for them no options exist. The code remains the basis for the warrior's actions in battle; if the leader is present, his movements become the measure for every venture throughout all levels of the action.

Ivanhoe suggests that chivalry properly defines the province of the upper classes, but in fact it can inspire heroic souls from the ranks. "For as the leader is, so will his followers be" (314). He sees the merits of chivalry, as a defining mode of conduct, without the need for clarification or possibility of doubt. Though physically incapable of joining the fight, Ivanhoe is by his very nature loyal to king and country; intellect and emotion here are one. He responds to the high destiny he associates with chivalry; battle calls out to him in a powerful language of approval. "I swear by the honour of my house—I vow by the name of my bright lady love, I would endure ten years' captivity to fight one day by that good knight's side in such a quarrel as this!" (317). Such approval inheres in the fact that this war against Norman corruption, and the unbalanced world order of which it is cause, is a good and necessary action. Scott may make some allowance for the knight's wound, but generally Ivanhoe's near hysteria as he responds to Rebecca's reports serves Scott's purpose quite well. The atmosphere becomes tense as the commentary between Ivanhoe and Rebecca shifts from an apparent review of Saxon tactics to the moral benefits gained in "the honest business" of fighting.

Scott's reservations about chivalry, however, had been made clear in a long essay for the *Encyclopedia Britannica* in 1818. Criticizing its fanaticism, superstition, and extravagance, he found it an often absurd system corrupted by its arbitrary choice of one or two virtues practiced to such an excessive degree as to become vices. Common standards of law and order were set aside. In military matters, a love of war for its own sake came to overwhelm even the true cause for which a war might be waged. Still, as much as Scott regretted these defects, he felt strongly that "nothing could be more beautiful and praiseworthy than the theory on which it is grounded."[28]

Ivanhoe reflects this emotional and intellectual ambivalence—the sorrow that so exquisite an ideal is unattainable. Most people assume that because Scott captured the sense of the Middle Ages vividly and took such pleasure in describing its settings and sounds, he had an uncritical view of chivalry. Nothing could be further from the truth. On at least one level *Ivanhoe* is, in fact, a chivalric debate: the old ethos is, as we have seen, scrutinized from several perspectives. Scott's method was to bring this debate into the present, where his contemporaries might study closely various models of chivalric behavior for their own instruction. Rebecca and Ivanhoe debate the medieval enthusiasms for knight-errantry in terms that the nineteenth-century man and woman might use to better understand their present system of manners.

Ivanhoe's sense of duty requires constant vigilance against those who would challenge his courage or through ignorance would misunderstand its virtues. "The love of battle is the food upon which we live," he argues, "the duty of the melee is the breath of our nostrils" (317). War was a matter of honor, and only those trained in the chivalric code, excluding women and clergy, could appreciate the moral benefits of manliness and self-sacrificing heroism. "Such, maiden, are the laws of chivalry . . . to which we offer all that we hold dear" (317).

The suspense of this moment builds not because of the terrific battle roaring outside, though the reader can hardly ignore it, but because one senses that the real issues of the novel have finally surfaced as ideas worthy of discussion. For all his emphasis on the point of the sword, Scott seems more taken with the intellectual and moral struggle between these two very different protagonists.

Rebecca, horrified by Ivanhoe's incapacity for soul searching, mocks his striving for glory and high destiny. She correctly perceives the anxiety in Ivanhoe's voice; his words confuse religious obligation with thoughts of impurity and justice with killing. Shocked that the man she respects, even loves, can blindly embrace personal glory above public good, Rebecca upbraids him: "What remains to you as the prize of all the blood you have spilled, of all the travail and pain you have endured, of all the tears which your deeds have caused?" (317). Thus the essential question is asked and, because it is so, another kind of trumpet blast sounds in the narrative. Though Ivanhoe is forced not only to answer Rebecca but also to face the bitter result of his impetuous idealism, Scott means implicitly to interrogate, also, the contemptible Prince John and his cohorts, as well as (finally) King Richard, who has misused his reign by pursuing his own interests while ignoring the suffering of his people.

Instinctively, Ivanhoe displays chivalry's best elements: physical strength, bravery, and courtesy, though he is not discerning of its defects. Rebecca, on the other hand, is far more critical. Personifying (as she sometimes does) Scott's scholarly imagination, she reflects the eighteenth-century view of chivalry as an outmoded, absurd system. Her view, however, does not predominate: neither Rebecca nor Ivanhoe achieve a victory in the debate. The point here is the debate itself. Charge and countercharge provoke our acceptance of Scott's view that the world is undergoing a process of improvement. If Ivanhoe is to have a significant role in the new society, he must possess "the virtues of the heart" as well as prove capable of more meaningful thought.

After we discover that Ivanhoe embraces knighthood merely to attain more glory, the depths of his refined selfishness become obvious. Rebecca struggles with the necessity of reshaping him; she knows that he should value clarity and reason more. "Glory is the rusted mail which hangs . . . over the champion's . . . tomb, is the defaced sculpture of the inscription which the ignorant monk can hardly read to the inquiring pilgrim—are these sufficient rewards . . . for a life spent miserably that ye may make others miserable?" (317–18), she asks. Feeling sorry for himself, contemptible even, Ivanhoe nonetheless resorts to the classic defense that chivalry is the best ethos for defining the aristocracy: the chivalric code distinguishes the aristocrat from everyone else. The privilege of bearing arms and aspiring to knighthood must remain, in Ivanhoe's view, an exclusive right of their estate.

Warming to the notion, Ivanhoe extends this essentially sociopolitical issue into the moral realm of men, and then into the religious. "Thou art no Christian," he tells Rebecca, "and to thee are unknown those high feelings which swell the bosom of a noble maiden when her lover hath done some deed of emprize which sanctions his flame" (318). Ivanhoe, quite naturally, caps his argument on a definition of chivalry and its virtues. With the battle raging outside and Rebecca's sharp-tongued criticisms finding their mark, he resorts to the traditional cure for a sick society—ecclesiastical and secular forces must join together. The ruling classes will rely on chivalric values as their guide. The dynamic forces in this new society, made obvious in the metaphor of battle, can be harnessed, according to Ivanhoe, through the subversion of human vice and the maintenance of peace and justice. True knighthood, the first and most enduring flower of a hard-pressed aristocracy, remains the best protection for English society as a whole. "Nobility were but an empty name without her, and liberty finds the best protection in her lance and sword" (318).

Our real education as readers continues when we, along with a disappointed Rebecca, sense the need to discuss other people accurately, no matter the mask of their words. Rebecca refuses to be insulted by Ivanhoe's language, though she has every reason to be; she dismisses all thought of leaving him to the protection of Chivalry. Instead, she still can love the good man in Ivanhoe while mourning his blindness as a characteristic prejudice of knight-errantry. Contemporary readers, under Scott's direction, may only be slightly less sympathetic. Ivanhoe, by training and temperament, belongs to the old order where simple chivalric virtues are sufficient armor for survival in a traditional world. But the England to which he returns has undergone new stresses that have visibly altered the *realpolitik*. The new test of those of ability and intelligence is whether they will adjust to the new nationalism, often initiated by commoners, or will isolate themselves, cloaked in traditional forms, from daily life.

Ivanhoe has given us a partial answer, not fully satisfying yet somewhat encouraging. He has fought to protect Rotherwood, not only the house of his father but also the place where his other family, Gurth and Wamba, live. While he offers the usual social and religious arguments, he has protected Isaac and Rebecca and been grateful for their protection of him. Now, ties of blood and self-interest become further complicated; rivalry between the classes increases as the battle for Torquilstone ends. War (quasi-revolution) has, in the absence of a strong monarch, upset the timetable for change—much has been destroyed, as well as gained. Ivanhoe, who falls asleep just before the final assault, will awaken to a new order. The question becomes whether or not he can, while caring for the welfare of his country, appreciate the virtues of the evolving commonwealth.

REFORMING THE SYSTEM

The sleeping Ivanhoe serves as an appropriate metaphor for the providential force of Rebecca. Her words have a humanizing effect, calming and silencing his warrior voice. As his nurse, she has treated not only his physical wounds but also his psychic injuries. Thus, while the battle rages outside the castle, Rebecca has won the war of words with *Ivanhoe*: he accepts peace. Scott has followed his principle of education: that is, the teacher should not protect students from making mistakes but allow them a full measure of error, while still guiding them as they seek the appropriate patterns of life. If Ivanhoe's self-will and romantic individualism can be tempered, Rebecca knows that he can serve as an ideal model of personal conduct, an inspiration in public life. Yet, to an increasing degree, Scott punishes those knights who fail to live up to the ideals of their oath.

While Rebecca advocates compromise and reconciliation, a parallel scene unfolds as Ulrica nurses the mortally wounded Front-de-Boeuf with an opposite intention. This Saxon daughter of Torquilstone, whose family was slaughtered and who has become the de Boeufs' mistress-slave, now vengefully tortures the injured Norman. "Think on thy sins, Reginald Front-de-Boeuf, . . . on rebellion, on rapine, on murder" (326). Unremorseful, de Boeuf sees nothing wrong in such ignominy; for him the ruling caste is entitled to its enjoyment of such spoils. The Normans perpetuate their power by oppressing the common Saxons, and in de Boeuf's view all Ulrica's protestations to the contrary are moot. But the contamination of Torquilstone castle extends beyond even these sins, to parricide, "the crime de la crime for Scott" (Wilt, 42). Ulrica, who has encouraged the parricide, now completes the circle with a symbolic killing of her father: she destroys his house with fire. "That secret I [Front-de-Boeuf] deemed locked in my own breast, and in that of one besides—the temptress, the partaker of my guilt" (327).

Scott maintains his radical focus on the necessity for historical change, yet he never loses sight of the damage done to individuals by that process. Before the providential arrival of Richard and Locksley, these parallel scenes (Rebecca/Ulrica) have shown quite clearly the problematic quality of change. Individuals remain fragile, vulnerable in the face of great historical movement, and too often no one anticipates the amount of human suffering left in its wake. Scott's refusal to idealize the past, together with his lack of confidence in the present society's capacity for progress, points up his increasing doubts about the future. The anxieties that remain after Richard's victory (and all the "green boughs glitter[ing] with . . . pearls of dew" cannot obscure them) anticipate the dramatic tension of the last third of the novel. The failure to retrieve Rebecca from her kidnapper and the continued passivity of *Ivanhoe*, who, having been saved at Templestowe, now disappears into a nearby priory for nine chapters, suggests the unresolved mysteries at the heart of the novel.

But for a moment these mysteries can be made to seem unimportant, when compared with the final scene of this section. Here, trust, equanimity, and mutual respect appear restored in the famous council episode between Richard and Locksley held underneath a great oak within sight of the destroyed Norman castle. Locksley has been dealing out justice and good sense to Normans and Saxons alike, managing even compassionate advice for Isaac. Richard, who has had the same opportunity to observe the results of humane behavior, can only express "his surprise at . . . so much civil policy amongst persons cast out" from law. "Good fruit, Sir Knight," avers Robin Hood, "will sometimes grow on a sorry tree . . . there are, doubtless, numbers who wish to exercise . . . with some moderation, and some who regret . . . they are obliged to follow such a trade at all" (375). If Richard can be educated to the real needs of his people, then he will understand the outlaws' desire to rejoin a lawful society and to swear fealty to their king.

Nearly two decades after the publication of *Ivanhoe* this was the meeting that inspired the Irish painter Daniel Maclise, whose *Robin Hood and His Merry Men Entertaining Richard Coeur de Lion in Sherwood Forest* went on exhibition at the Royal Academy in 1839. Aside from his genuine enthusiasm for chivalry, Maclise was reflecting a political philosophy that hated utilitarianism as well as the laissez-faire economics that had (in his view) ruined England. He believed the duty of both government and the aristocracy was to protect the working classes from the excesses of tyrannical ministers or factory owners. Their lives and the nation could not be left to the whim of God and Nature. His paintings, especially *Robin Hood and His Merry Men,* show the highest virtues of chivalry uncorrupted and a joyous celebration when individuals from all classes mingle without concern for status or position. Had Scott seen this painting, he would have appreciated the richness of Maclise's composition and the brilliancy of his colors, but not Maclise's denial (he would have felt) of the underlying pessimism, the implication that real tragedy may be so fortuitously averted. Maclise is all happy-endings; Scott finds nothing in the chivalric ethos so simplistic, so certain.

7

Templestowe Corrupted

The movement toward cultural reconciliation and continuity undergoes a further severe test in the final third of the novel. Not surprisingly, Rebecca remains the chief agent of decency; she serves as the novel's
moral focus, casting into sharp relief *Ivanhoe*'s fidelity and Bois-
Guilbert's nihilism, Richard's providential humanity and John's fatal-
ism. Ever articulate, she sounds the theme fully: "It cannot be that in
merry England, the hospitable, the generous, the free, where so many
are ready to peril their lives for honour, there will not be found one to
fight for justice" (424). Estranged and dispossessed, accused falsely of
witchcraft by the corrupt Templar, Rebecca pleads meaningfully and
memorably; she marks the continuing instability of English life.

Her present circumstance, however—she is the prisoner of the
Lucas de Beaumanoir, Grand Master of the Templars at Templestowe—
makes apparent her inability as a protagonist to change things. Her call
for justice, as one of a vulnerable minority, sounds even more plain-
tively than the cries of the Saxon peasants who have suffered under the
Norman yoke. Evidence of radicalism and revolution is everywhere;
some, like Locksley, have rebelled outright, though, except for
Torquilstone, such dissent benefits only a radicalized minority (out-

laws). But Locksley's "true English" spirit has its own mysterious powers for affirming order; he lends himself neither to an easy understanding nor simplification. For Scott no one character can serve as an effective agent of change. Ivanhoe, still weak from his wounds at Ashby, recovers at a monastery, far from the action. His inactivity once again suggests his continued, symbolic despondency—alone and disinherited from the new, emerging national order.

This loss of confidence and assertiveness disappears with Richard's arrival at the priory. Typically, his notion of kingship allows for little beyond a few well-chosen words and a quick departure: always he pursues individual adventure at some distant place. The effect on Ivanhoe, however, is a recharging of his physical and intellectual powers. As the King passes into "the shades of the surrounding forest" (450), Ivanhoe senses once again the organic life and power of the nation, embodied not in Richard but in the whole environment and time. Seeing the King causes Ivanhoe to think usefully about the dangers facing England and its people. He asks the prior (his spiritual advisor), "Have you never found your mind darkened, like the sunny landscape, by the sudden cloud, which augurs a coming tempest?" (451). Thinking out loud, he convinces himself that such "hints" are deserving of attention.

Nothing shows as effectively as does this scene the growing desire of men like Ivanhoe and Locksley (and less conclusively Richard) to accept reality. Individuality and knight-errantry cannot secure the new order. When Ivanhoe goes riding after Richard, he begins answering Rebecca's earlier question ("are these sufficient rewards . . . ?") in a new manner. This is not the Ivanhoe of Ashby; the horrors and lessons of Torquilstone and the forced isolation of St. Botolph's priory have proved that civil war exacts a terrible cost. If he can blunt the reaction of his Saxon brothers at Coningsburgh to Richard's arrival, Ivanhoe may encourage justice and peace among Normans and Saxons. Scott gives credence to such a view when the old prior wryly comments as he watches the young knight ride into the forest, "as great men forget little men's service, truly I shall hold me well repaid in having done that which is right . . . in the good cause of Old England" (453).

Locksley, who has already shown his capacity as hero-manager, retains a near mystical influence on the infuriatingly romantic Richard. The King, whom Scott clearly finds both compelling and yet often foolish, gambols through the forest singing songs, engaging in repartee with the jester (Wamba), and expressing "careless gaiety and fearless confidence." His is "a mind which was unapt to apprehend danger, and prompt to defy it when most imminent" (454). This attitude clouds Richard's vision of reality and confirms his own inability to take corrective action alone, whether it is to recognize the signs of an imminent ambush or the collapse of his monarchy.

Wamba enjoys the freedom of a court jester by warning Richard and mocking him for his insufficiencies. Playing upon the stereotype of king and jester, Wamba seemingly confuses the two roles in joking about "valour and folly . . . once more boon companions" (460). Clearly he distrusts Richard's unwillingness to take precautions, even to the point of persuading the King to release Locksley's horn (given as a mark of the yeoman's fidelity) so that in case of attack a rescue call can be sounded. When the inevitable ambush occurs, Richard—quite as inevitably—fights against overwhelming odds, and only Wamba's trumpet blast brings in Locksley and his band a much-needed deliverance. Again Richard is forced to resign himself to the help of an unofficial counselor. Richard remains a brave, generous warrior who has readily sensed the deep divisions within his kingdom, yet his education has not fully instilled the notion of a responsible aristocracy. He has come far toward accepting rational and reconciling values, but alone without his counselors, Ivanhoe and Locksley, Richard drifts back into a more capricious life.

"UNDER EVERY GREEN TREE"

A recent critic has argued that in Scott's novels there is a borderline between "some version of ancient and modern times."[29] Along such a border, conflicts naturally arise; as Scott addresses this theme in *Ivanhoe,* the forces of modernity must win if England is to survive. But the past has virtues that should not be lost in the struggle, nor should the future be seen as free from doubt and anxiety. Progressivism requires that distinctions between good and evil, present and past, realism and romance, be clearly marked. Scott's presentation demands, however, more subtlety and awareness: he blurs the borderlines and complicates the dramatic conflicts. Why else would he deliberately undermine our respect and admiration for Richard's reconciling humanity?

Immediately after defeating the ambushers, sent by his brother Prince John and led by the ambitious Waldemar Fitzurse, Richard, with Locksley at his side, questions his chief attacker. "What could urge one of thy rank and seeming worth to so foul an undertaking?" (463), a query that speaks to Scott's divided sympathies regarding aristocratic and middle-class values. The answer comes in mocking tones—"thou knowest little of mankind . . . [I] avenge on thee thy disobedience to thy father"—thus jolting Richard into accepting the harsh realities that some of his own courtiers may despise him and that his brother seeks to usurp his throne. What remains is how the King will decide the fate of the traitor Fitzurse. Richard's actions here prove he is a prince of compassion as well as one sometimes capable of good political sense. Unwilling to kill the corrupt Fitzurse, he banishes him from England and prevents Locksley from taking vengeance against him.

Richard first appears in *Ivanhoe* dressed entirely in black, bearing no coat-of-arms or sign to identify him. He has been disinherited—lost his throne—and in effect become nameless. But in sparing Fitzurse, in this signal act of humanity and charity, he moves swiftly to identify himself to his valued counselor. "Thou bearest an English heart, Locksley . . . I am Richard of England" (464). With the talisman word, "English," Richard, showing the colors of mourning and loss, reunites with his heritage. The result anticipates the eventual communing of different races and ranks under one banner, but as Locksley here suggests (as he has earlier), such a synthesis cannot be easily accomplished or a conflict necessarily mediated at the order of one man.

The problem lies in the fact that Locksley is neither purely a hero nor an utter villain. Richard, romantic and anachronistic, thinks in terms of the heroic ideal and has no real understanding of the heroic actions of common men joined in a noble cause. Wamba develops the idea: "those honest fellows balance a good deed with one not quite so laudable . . . the merry men of the forest set off the building of a cottage with the burning of castle" (458–59). Critics have referred to Scott's technique here as the "deflation of romantic heroism" or "the mystery of outlawry"; both views seem at least partially correct. By the end of this section Scott may simply be expressing a thoughtful, mature reflection on the nature of self-hood. Locksley represents the unconquered democratic spirit, mysterious and unknowable. His is a natural nobility, superior in many ways to that of more conventional heroes. Yet there exists a coincidental irony of management here. As successful as he is in directing the eventual reconciliation, Locksley ends up separated from those he has brought back into power.

CEREMONY AND DOUBTS

Deliverance remains an essential characteristic of the last chapters of *Ivanhoe*. When Locksley rescues Richard from the ambush, this is, of course, an actual, physical deliverance; the kingdom apparently is restored to its rightful king. The health of the nation seems secure. Or is it? For Scott, the larger meaning of Richard's rescue and the subsequent ceremonial feast, which the recently arrived Ivanhoe attends, is not yet fully articulated. He has begun to resolve his themes and tie off plot leads, but as a historian he still has to come to terms with the restoration of traditional authority.

Scott lived during a period when authority was in crisis, Francis Hart has shown, and his conception of that crisis pervades his novels. "The authority appealed to is often unreliable and irresponsible; it must be recreated before it can function effectively and legitimately" (Hart 1978, 52). As we have seen, the figures of authority in *Ivanhoe* are indeed unreliable as well as divisive. Humane action and diplomacy do rescue authority from total confusion, but Scott clearly undercuts the new order. He allows for realistic qualification of the romantic ideal by, for example, having Ivanhoe debate with Richard on equal terms. Jokingly, Richard accuses Ivanhoe of disloyalty for not remaining in the priory as ordered (469–70); Ivanhoe brusquely ignores the

King's playfulness and launches into a passionate diatribe on the dangers of knight-errantry. Refusing to understand the seriousness of this speech, the King feels only pride in having achieved "an adventure with only his good sword, and his good arm" (470). What is more frustrating to Ivanhoe is the King's inability to be other than comic and vain. Unusually assertive, Ivanhoe has a revelation of sorts: "But your kingdom my Liege,—your kingdom is threatened with dissolution and civil war; your subjects menaced with every species of evil, if deprived of their sovereign in some of those dangers which it is your daily pleasure to incur and from which you have but this moment narrowly escaped" (470).

Ivanhoe's reeducation has taken effect, for he can now sometimes distinguish public responsibility from individual feelings. By encouraging Richard to distinguish between disorder and order, lies and truth, Ivanhoe reveals his own increasing credibility as a leader in the new society, and by contrast Richard's inadequacy for the long term. For as the omniscient narrator feels obliged to add, "his reign was like the course of a brilliant and rapid meteor, shedding around an unnecessary . . . light . . . instantly swallowed up by universal darkness . . . affording none of those solid benefits to his country on which history loves to pause, and hold up as an example to posterity" (471–72). Both the major characters and the narrator will here challenge the concept of traditional authority: is it only a fantasy, an illusory display?

One faces the ending of the novel with real apprehension; all references to achieving lasting peace and harmony take on an ironic bitterness, the theme of mismanagement surveyed in quite uncompromising terms. But, as if sensing that his melancholy may have peaked too soon, Scott returns to the forest feast and the triangular gathering of hero-managers (Ivanhoe and Locksley), King Richard, and the omniscient narrator, who meet symbolically beneath a huge oak tree.

We are expected to meditate on Richard's bravery and kindness as a monarch. We must try to do so—difficult as this may be. It requires no effort to reflect upon what fine subjects he has. There is something compelling and attractive about Locksley and Ivanhoe. Responsible, intelligent, insightful, they are men of tenacious faith—

resolved to come together as one in mutual interdependence, trust, and admiration. Their character, more than Richard's, explains the victories at Ashby, Torquilstone, and, finally, Templestowe. Richard himself grows more appealing as he grows in kindness; though recklessness often prevails, Ivanhoe and Locksley, his agents of providence, define the moral value of leadership.

Richard's address to Locksley and Ivanhoe legitimates their management of him (and the state). He first calls Locksley "The King of Sherwood" and publicly announces "thou art right." Again, in a later speech, he refers to both men as good and right in their actions, though he chafes at the knowledge of having "as little the freedom of mine own will as any king in Christendom" (474). Through selective disobedience and shrewd direction, Ivanhoe and Locksley restore the bond of *comitatus* with the assistance of Richard's "good intentions." In Scott's nineteenth-century crisis view, the King no longer serves as a reliable figure of authority: instead, Richard merely impersonates such a figure. "The wise and attentive precautions" of his managers save the kingdom, though we are not allowed to forget how such a reconciliation is tempered by "the king's untimely death" (475).

REVELATIONS AT CONINGSBURGH CASTLE

Richard is a king who embodies danger, death, and the power of enchantment. Little wonder, therefore, that men of diverse backgrounds and differing motivations, Ivanhoe and Locksley, should more than willingly become his disciples. Paradoxically, however, Richard's followers must stand apart from his adventurism and act as responsible moral agents. Without the independent action of these singular individuals, society will remain impoverished in spirit and fortune. Scott clarifies further Ivanhoe's and Locksley's prudent decisions in the forest by playing out the entanglements, not only of their relationship to the quixotic King, but also their strategy for redeeming the future, in the public world of the great Norman castles.

Coningsburgh Castle symbolizes the power of the conquerors over the conquered. "A royal residence of the kings of England,"

Coningsburgh bears its Saxon origin even in its name, but its more recent outer walls are clearly of Norman origin, its Saxon antiquity no more than picturesque. Scott suggests that his characters must sort out the various forces represented here. To make any sense of the muddle of these architectural styles—ancient and modern, obsolete and improved, orderly and chaotic—these human beings, Saxon and Norman alike, must struggle for perception without having the intellectual detachment or chronological distance necessary to see the progress of history. Uncertainty, as Daniel Cottom says, remains a constant in their lives, and they feel "helpless before essentially impersonal forces responsible to no order of reason, progress, or truth" (133).

The circumstances of Richard's arrival at Coningsburgh suggest the confusion and disharmony so prevalent in these human relationships. The King has come to attend Athelstane's "funeral" and, more significantly, to effect a reconciliation between Cedric and Ivanhoe. With this long-awaited denouement, the novel seems well on its way to the final reconciliation between the opposing forces; but Scott implies that there may be no rational, orderly conclusion. The heads of the most important Saxon families present, Cedric and Richard preside at Athelstane's "wake," ostensibly honoring the Saxon prince. But the funeral also serves as the occasion when Richard identifies himself to Cedric and invites the Saxons to accept his "equal protection." Here the conventional romance formula of death ushering in new life or reborn hope comes into play. The superficial nobility of the scene lasts only through Ivanhoe's reconciliation with his father, and then the ideology of the narrative takes an unexpected turn with Athelstane's "resurrection from the dead."

The Saxon cause, embodied as it is in Athelstane's potential as the new Saxon hero, now truly seems at an end—dying not in some noble and clarifying way, but anticlimactically given up in Cedric's empty dreams and Athelstane's foolish return. Athelstane's return to life reaffirms the ambivalence of the Saxon cause and undercuts Richard's providential efforts at unity. In a curious way, this event foreshadows the ambivalence the reader feels at the end of the novel toward restorative authority. Scott forces us to come to terms with the failed Cedric in ourselves, the necessity (as he must see) of sacrificing strongly held personal beliefs for the greater good: the importance of giving up foolish dreams for practical reality and destiny. Paradoxically, we then must realize that even with a transfer of one's allegiance to the new figure, no guarantee exists. Security and effectiveness do not necessarily follow.

The ideal of the *Waverley* Novels remains the achievement of an ordered, peaceful society where all serve and are protected by a just system of law. The failure of Cedric here is predictable on two counts: his use of disorder as a vehicle for supplanting the Normans with a Saxon prince, and his reliance on the oafish, sluggard Athelstane, known as "the Unready." Cedric resorts to the active dissolution of the bonds between father and son, king and subject, citizen and citizen. Even after he acknowledges the presence of King Richard and embraces the newly reconciled Ivanhoe, he still speaks of Athelstane's duty to regain the throne of Alfred, King of the Saxons. But none of the central party remains to hear Cedric's ramblings. Ivanhoe and Richard leave for their final reckoning, and Rowena, now released from a false marriage proposal, can devote her full attention to planning a secure home and homecoming for her true knight.

DESTRUCTION OF THE TEMPLE

The final crisis, much anticipated and profoundly suggestive of Scott's sanity, settles the fate of Rebecca, while it rids us, also, of Bois-Guilbert. Ivanhoe, who first appeared as a dark form lying at the foot of a cross, and who comes into the light at Ashby and (less clearly) at Torquilstone, now enters the dark, dangerous confines of Templestowe. Sensing the mood of the crowd, "the hour when the bloody die was to be cast for the life or death of Rebecca," the mob's "earnest desire [was] to look on blood and death . . . they were habituated to the bloody spectacle of brave men falling" (494). Scott underlines the satanic nature of the Templars' slaves, ready to burn the witch, like demons employing diabolical exercises, showing "their white fangs" to the startled villagers. "They whispered to each other, and communicated all the feats which Satan had performed during that busy and unhappy period"

(495). The effect of this description is highly visual. We can imagine the fear and loathing of the mob as it pushes forward to view the accused. Such epithets as "fatal circle," "horrible duty," and "the sullen sounds" display Scott's particular genius for enforcing the awful, darkening the gloomy, and aggravating the dreadful (to paraphrase Samuel Johnson).

Our attention is on Rebecca, in particular on the solitary aspect of her condition—once again, her role as the moral agent of the novel has center stage. Her words, her actions, have the greatest credibility, because she suffers most acutely for her compassion and tolerance. The distortion of her character, the exaggeration of her religious beliefs, heaped upon her by the Templars, have only sharpened our sense of their rampant prejudice and religious bigotry. *Ivanhoe*, who has learned from Rebecca's example, acts swiftly to free her, but ultimately lacks the emancipated spirit necessary to declare his commitment to the ideals she represents. His human limitations prevent him from fully embracing Rebecca's nobility, even at its most splendid moment.

Her chief accuser, Lucas Beaumanoir, suffers from a heart hardened by blind attachment to the supreme power he enjoys so much. His manner and method stand in contrast to those of Richard, whose every action may be, on one level, motivated by his love of adventure but whose ultimate motivation remains providential. Ironically, the Grand Master Beaumanoir takes pleasure in comparing himself to a "kind shepherd" who protects his flock against "the raging wolf." His only true instinct is, however, for the consolidation of his power through further intimidation and fear mongering.

Scott levels his greatest scorn on those fanatics and demagogues who promote chaos and civil war. As a moral psychologist, he probes matters of conscience. Beaumanoir, whose mission in England is to reassert the power of his Order, stands in ironic contrast to Richard yet is the ecclesiastical twin of Cedric. His character reveals moral imbalance, lack of judgment, perversion of truth, and rigid inhumanity.[30] In his insanity he exemplifies the "life-denying," as opposed to Ivanhoe, Richard, and Locksley, who typify the "life-fulfilling." Beaumanoir's presence threatens both group and individual: "Even in our own days, when morals are better understood, an execution, a bruising-match, a riot, or a meeting of radical reformers, collects . . . immense crowds of spectators . . . to see how matters are to be conducted" (494).

The ignorance, prejudice, and likely viciousness of the mob seem clear, as does their reason for assembling—the fire-brand Lucas. The monastic culture that produced him must take its full responsibility in Scott's world. Beaumanoir's pride, "the conscious dignity and imaginary merit of the part" he would play in saving the world from evil, required his suppression of every human feeling that might interfere with his perception of duty. Thus his conversion of vice into virtue mirrors that of Bois-Guilbert. Instead of leading the Knight Templar away from the destructive spirits, Beaumanoir only deepens his depression and cynicism.

Bois-Guilbert, who at first hoped to gain Rebecca's affection by force, now opposes any effort to harm her. His own passions remain confused, so much so that he feels only scorn and indignation for Beaumanoir's plan to use Rebecca as a scapegoat for the lost ambitions of the Templars. As Bois-Guilbert removes his moral blinders and becomes more observant, he struggles between spiritual stultification and spiritual fruition. With a sublime pathos, he strains to explain himself to Rebecca: "Dost thou hear me? Dost thou understand my words? The sound of my voice is frightful in mine own ears. I scarce know on what ground we stand, or for what purpose they have brought us hither" (502). His pleading has only the veneer of truth and cannot withstand Rebecca's perceptive gaze. "My mind and senses keep truth and time. . . . Tempter, begone! . . . I hold thee as my worst and most deadly enemy" (503). He defines life and liberty in terms repugnant to her. Rebecca's ethical resolve, her willingness to die before repudiating her religion, and her continuing didactic role make it impossible for her to respond to his offer of "a new world of pleasure."

Feminist readings of Rebecca's role would show how the men in the novel, including Ivanhoe, see her as an agent of an alien world, purposefully evoking anger and hatred. Yet Rebecca sees men as long-suffering defenders of an indefensible order. The conspiracy of all the men here (Isaac and Ivanhoe are implicated), resulting in Rebecca's near execution and final departure from England, issues from their anxiety and fear as she struggles to reinvent the traditional discourse.

In periods of great cultural insecurity, when the fear of social anarchy and perhaps even of civil war exist, the longing for strict controls—of gender, race, religion—intensifies.[31] If individuals can be kept in their proper spheres (those established by church and crown, sustained by faith and fear), society may be preserved and the inevitability of change made more bearable. Rebecca's attack on chivalry, together with her attempt to alter the prostrate Ivanhoe's idealized view of chivalric conduct, elicits the sexual antagonism in the novel. Ivanhoe suffers a crisis of masculinity as he increasingly realizes that the code by which he defines himself is threatened; their mutual attraction, already complicated by the issue of interracial love, only heightens his male resentment of this independent woman. This battle between the sexes comes into play again, for example, when Bois-Guilbert kidnaps Rebecca at the moment of her rescue (an image of psychosexual pleasure); the threat of sexual danger is pervasive. He brings her to the Temple, this enclave of men's professional brotherhood, to demonstrate his power, his prowess in the complementary interplay of dominance and subordination.

The turbulence and corruption of Norman Ashby and Saxon Torquilstone are revisited in the Christian Templestowe. With anarchy imminent, the Temple threatened, the reformer Beaumanoir decides to establish strict border controls. The anarchy represented in the actions of Bois-Guilbert and Rebecca must be crushed. "To this can the light look of woman, aided by the Prince of Powers of this world, bring a valiant and worthy knight . . . we spit at and defy the foul enemy," he proclaims (412). Beaumanoir's call for a cleansing death to free the Temple and restore the new Jerusalem predictably falls upon the one woman whose every action in the novel has been toward just such healing. As Judith Wilt notes, "the value of healing which [Rebecca] represents is a value for the waking, wounded, world" (45).

Rebecca's struggle, interrupted by Ivanhoe's rescue, marks a consummation of their attraction for each other. The power of her healing arts, always a providential force in the novel, has quieted Ivanhoe's earlier sexual hysteria. Actually, he arrives at Coningsburgh weak, weary, and "scarce able to support himself in the saddle" (504). Depleted of sexual energy and still struggling with his identity, Ivanhoe seeks both Rebecca and Bois-Guilbert to find a kind of finality and answer.

This journey into the self, arguably the dominant metaphor of the novel, concludes in a pseudo-marriage ceremony. Ivanhoe defines himself in language evocative of the marriage oath: "I am a good knight and noble come to sustain the just and lawful quarrel of this damsel . . . against [the] false and truthless . . . Bois-Guilbert" (504). After stating his name for the record, he approaches Rebecca asking her to marry him. "Dost thou accept of me for thy champion?"; notably, he would be her "champion." She readily answers three times "I do," thus irrevocably confirming her acceptance; since Ivanhoe is "the champion whom Heaven hath sent me," she avows (505). All that remains is to remove the godless Bois-Guilbert, whose real crime is less his exploitation of Rebecca than his emotional betrayal of Ivanhoe, his implicit violation of their chivalric male bonding. His death purifies the putative "marriage," and the ceremony concludes with the priest Beaumanoir's blessing, "This is indeed the judgement of God" (506).

Behind the irony of Richard's kingship, behind the irony of Robin of Locksley's disappearance into the trees, exists the final irony of Ivanhoe's double "marriages." His "marriage" here to Rebecca and his imminent marriage to Rowena are also illustrative of his essential duality, the split between his imagination and reality itself. The argument that for Ivanhoe Rebecca is not a flesh-and-blood woman but an idealized figure of gentleness is insufficient.

Obviously, an actual marriage cannot have taken place, for Ivanhoe consciously loves Rowena; his faithful, selfless devotion to her makes any other prospect impossible. Subconsciously, however, his alter-ego, intimated quite persuasively in his exchange of fathers, Cedric for Richard, and in his several inconclusive battles with Bois-Guilbert, could marry Rebecca; in Ivanhoe's imagination, their union is plausible. The ethical bond the two have forged—before Ashby, during Torquilstone, and now in the Temple—gives increased significance to the spiritual and mystical affinities they share. With Rebecca,

Ivanhoe must look into his heart of darkness; not surprisingly, he turns away from what he sees there, and seeks a more affirming image (wife), sunny and domestic. Rowena will marry Ivanhoe, her idealistic view of him intact; his memories of chivalrous combat will be untainted by further criticism.

Cultural reconciliation is thus achieved and the disinherited regain their birthright. But at what cost—Rebecca is set free only to be sacrificed emotionally, exiled in Spain where she remains mute and celibate. While thus Scott does not fully support the feminist ideological position, he does feel the pain of women's frustration as they struggle against a mechanistic society.

FINAL SCENES

After the startling death of Bois-Guilbert, who has succumbed to "the violence of his own contending passions" (506), and with Ivanhoe's refusal to accept the traditional chivalric reward—the arms and corpse of his dead opponent—a new order, cognizant of the abuses of the past, is symbolically urged into place. Richard's arrival signals the beginning of the end for the powerful Templars and their "dark line of spears." Civil and secular power, for the time being, hold sway over the defiant priests. Scott chooses not to settle the crisis between sovereign king and the Pope's minister, the Grand Master; instead, a stalemate, suggestive of the vulnerability inherent in peace, replaces open warfare.

Each party respects the other's courage, yet the Templars must acknowledge their defeat in being banished from Templestowe. The restored king disinherits the corrupt; the forces of progress overtake the Templars. Such too is the situation for Richard: the responsibility of kingship, which he finds impossible, is again his, and the moment of recovery is overtaken by the process of abandonment. Ivanhoe, who has redeemed his warrior soul once more, must now relinquish it for his new national role as well as for his emerging personal (and sexual) identity.

Scott portrays with superb artistry the complicated nature of these new obligations. His closing the novel with Rebecca and Rowena at center stage strikes exactly the right chord. On the second day after the marriage of Rowena and Ivanhoe, Rebecca visits Rowena. Though the two women have quite different backgrounds, they both love Ivanhoe. Rowena has long been drawn to him, and their marriage is the happy result of all her girlhood dreams. She accepts and trusts in him, and is also thankful for the clarity he brings to her and her world. Rowena's grasp of the new order—"my husband has favour with the King: the King himself is just and generous" (516)—shows a profound respect for tradition and, ironically, the past. For her the clash of loyalties has resulted in a purging of predatory tribalism and the establishment of an ordered society. Rebecca's love of Ivanhoe, on the other hand, is of more recent origin, a result, at least in part, of the stressful environment of Ashby and Torquilstone. Love, the most incendiary of feelings, may flourish in such places, though peace and serenity can secure no permanent hold. Rebecca remains unconvinced that the new order will succeed. "The people of England are a fierce race, quarrelling ever with their neighbors or among themselves, and ready to plunge the sword into the bowels of each other" (516).

Scott's stoic rationalism here pervades Rebecca's last words. Prejudice, as well as the religious and racial bigotry that have long been imbedded in the kingdom, still exist. The collisions of history, as Edgar Johnson has called them, between the forces of progress and the security of the past, between civilization and barbarism, continue even in the new society. No one man, even one as humane as Ivanhoe or as courageous as Richard, no love of a woman for a man—as Rebecca notes in Rowena's "tinge of the world's pride or vanities" (517)—can, in Scott's view, withstand or alter the great transformation of history.

Rebecca's leaving does not mean (necessarily) that she rejects the new order, only that her sense of realism will not permit her to indulge in its naivete. Her gift of jewels to the couple constitutes her final practical, as well as symbolic, effort to celebrate their marriage as well as to acknowledge their acceptance of a new national order. Though what happens to Rebecca and her father represents a great waste, their loss to England is caused not by their unwillingness to compromise their principles but by society's irrational prejudice. Scott also makes the point that even when social integration occurs, not everyone is reconciled; some will remain outside, victims of human cruelty.

For Scott, the self-exile of Rebecca is inextricably connected with the ignominious end of King Richard. His decision to go off on another crusade results in a series of tragedies, not the least of which is his premature death. "With the life of a generous, but rash and romantic, monarch perished all the projects which his ambition and his generosity had formed" (519). Sufficiently deflating the expected romantic ending, Scott concludes *Ivanhoe* with a quotation (slightly altered) from Samuel Johnson's "The Vanity of Human Wishes" (1748), the section referring to the tragic death of Charles XII of Sweden.

> He left the name at which the world grew pale.
> To point a moral, or adorn a TALE.

Scott fully grasps Johnson's satire and his strong affinities with stoic thought. The theme of Johnson's poem—the inability of the world to offer genuine satisfaction, and thus our need to turn from worldly life to seek joy in religious faith—is close to Scott's own conception of the human dilemma.

Scott attacks the emptiness of military glory; yet beyond the obvious, he also illumines the helpless vulnerability of the individual in the social realm.[32] The clash of impersonal forces, the tangled jungle of vanities and passions where men and women both innocent and evil may be ambushed—this essential theme, of course, suggests that *Ivanhoe* is, as critics have recently reminded us, like all of the Waverley Novels, only more so: ambivalent about the inevitable confrontation of classes and cultures; about the idealizing of ancient, traditional patterns of life; and about celebrating progress uncritically.

Like all great stories, the end of *Ivanhoe* has its own unique power. Scott's sympathy for human suffering and his admiration for the human capacity to love and respect idealism are portrayed with unerring skill. Certainly, Scott's doubts for the future are a response to his own quicksilver age, with its popular unrest, political radicalism, and struggle against Napoleon. *Ivanhoe* captures all this and more in a vehicle in which fascinating—even legendary—personalities from the English past provide the dramatic intrigue of this portrait of contemporary society.

8

Ivanhoe's Artistic Legacy

I have argued from the beginning of this study not only for the intrinsic value of *Ivanhoe* as a work of fiction but for its capacity to perfectly reflect the mood of its generation. As a recent Scott biographer writes, "In some nebulous way, [*Ivanhoe*] spoke for [its] time."[33] In trying to explain the mystery behind the novel's inspiring effect on readers, one must of course rely on the text and Scott's statements about his role as an artist: "no great poetic artist . . . ever presents a literal truth rather than the idealized image of a truth" ("Essay on Chivalry," 15). The spell of *Ivanhoe* becomes more evident when one accepts it as a projection of moral righteousness, an expression of how good art can rise above the merely ornamental, devising and refining an equitable system of change for the culture.

The notion that good art mirrors the existence of a just society was a firmly held belief among a number of nineteenth-century playwrights, composers, and painters. The social crises of the period demanded that works of art preserve the strengths of the past, while seeking new values, new formulas for expressing feelings. British and continental artists found in *Ivanhoe* the resources for expressing the ideals of national aspiration and identity. The Gothic revival and the cult of medievalism had, since 1750, bred an enthusiasm for escaping into the past and discovering ancient works, from James Macpherson's *Ossian* to Chatterton and Walpole, while creating a code of values for appreciating them. Historians and novelists alike had begun using examples from the past as proofs of present conditions. When Scott's *Ivanhoe* appeared, the book was a kind of didactic canon, complete with archetypal images of moral virtue, bravery, trust, and fidelity in its major characters; through these images Scott presses for the creation of a just social order.

These associations and predispositions became so firmly rooted in the nineteenth-century audience, in part because of *Ivanhoe's* vast popularity but also because of a thoroughgoing revival of the Arthurian legend, that British popular culture sought to satisfy its medievalizing desires in all the arts. Poetry and prose, melodramas and some legitimate drama, as well as plays with songs, musical interludes, a variety of scenic effects for the theater, and opera were affected. Later painting, architecture, sculpture, and the decorative arts began showing medieval influences. As Debra Mancoff makes clear, "The evolution of the Gothic Revival was enduring . . . and complex [but] not united by a singular, consistent aesthetic."[34]

While one approach to studying this evolution is to define a consistency of style, another and perhaps more fruitful one is to study one work as it reflects the attitude of a diverse group of artists whose intentions regarding the medieval inspiration are more significant than the actual result. By focusing on the nature of their interpretations of *Ivanhoe,* one can see how these artists read the novel's "symbols of the past as lessons in morals and virtue for the present" (Mancoff, 10).

One group of artists and playwrights found the literary conditions in the early nineteenth-century most unfavorable. Since the Licensing Act of 1737 was still in force, only two patent theaters, Drury Lane and Covent Garden, and the Opera House in the Haymarket could lawfully produce drama; other theaters were restricted to musical entertainments. By using songs, dance, pantomime, recitative, and incidental music, the dramatic nature of the plays tended toward the extreme, with often little regard for convincing motivation. These melodramas, however, kept audiences thrilled with emotional highs and lows, where very good characters are joyfully rewarded and very bad characters receive their just punishment, and all is concluded happily.

During the formative years of the unlicensed minor theaters, when melodramas grew even after the stubborn resistance from traditionalists, the adaptations of Scott novels took center stage. Though contemporary dramatic estimates were often erratic and remain so, their literary merit can be judged more effectively by comparing the dramas with the original novel.

London became the most popular location for *Waverley* romances, with theaters producing legitimate patents to the most garish musical travesties. At one point four *Ivanhoe*s, each emphasizing a different critical moment in the novel, were running in houses blocks from one another during the same month. The vogue of dramatic adaptations of *Ivanhoe* rose to such a height that one twentieth-century critic has exclaimed to his own amazement: "With the exception of two or three decades, every period of ten years has brought out an important version of *Ivanhoe*."[35]

A month before the publication of *Ivanhoe,* in a letter dated 10 November 1819, Scott had assured his good friend, the actor-producer Daniel Terry, who had earlier scored a success on the London stage with *Rob Roy* and *The Heart of Midlothian,* that the new novel would make a fine addition to his repertoire except that the "expense of scenery and decorations would be great, this being a tale of chivalry, not of character" (*Letters,* 6:10). Terry did not respond to this overture, but numerous others did.

Before 1850, the best-known adaptation was Thomas Dibdin's *Ivanhoe; or, the Jew's Daughter* appearing at the Surrey Theater on 20 January 1820, less than a month after the novel's publication. Aside from improving Bois-Guilbert's sense of gentlemanly propriety and moral conduct, Dibdin seems most concerned with what might be called the central dramatic moments: the natural beauties of Rotherwood, the knightly tournament at Ashby, the conviviality of Robin Hood and his men, the Torquilstone dungeon with Isaac mulling over his golden ransom, and the terrors of Rebecca, who may burn at the Templestowe stake.

Five imitations (actually, six, including Beazley's musical drama, which will be discussed later) followed in the same year; three of these efforts have a similar three-act structure. Alfred Bunn's compilation is marked with Wamba's rough but good-hearted humor and his early (and accepted) marriage proposal to Rowena's maid, Elgitha. Central to the tone of the piece is Robin's gleemen, who sing old English ballads, while keeping by way of comic contrast any concern over Bois-Guilbert's marauding band to a minimum. Act 2 finds the central characters imprisoned in Torquilstone, except *Ivanhoe* and Robin, who remain in Sherwood Forest. Rebecca must relate Bois-Guilbert's marriage proposal to her father, thus somewhat explaining the curious title of the play, *Ivanhoe; or, the Jew of York.* The final act has a wonderful forest court scene with *Ivanhoe*, Robin Hood, and his crew, who force Isaac to pay for his daughter's freedom as well as that of the other prisoners. In the meantime, Rebecca is captured once more and brought before the Grand Master, who condemns her to the stake. *Ivanhoe* finally appears as her champion and reaffirms her last refusal of Bois-Guilbert's proposal. Sword play follows and Brian dies, but in the final lines *Ivanhoe* speaks for the King, warning Templars and all who threaten England: "Beware! thou'rt in the lion's grasp!" The key difference between Bunn's play (and similar imitations) and the novel remains the dramatist's balancing of comic versus tragic material. While not distorting the novel, Bunn removes what some critics have found mechanical in the original.

Readers have always reflected on what Rebecca's future might have been if *Ivanhoe* had acknowledged his love for her. George Soane, in *The Hebrew,* stage production and published text out in 1820, is the earliest of a number of writers, Thackeray among them (in *Rebecca and Rowena* [1849]), who found a different answer to the dilemma of whether one welcomes an intelligent woman with resources of humor, courage, and loyalty or exiles her. Soane, who had a reputation for freely altering the storyline in Scott's novels, focuses on the growing friendship of Rebecca and *Ivanhoe.* The couple are at Rotherwood; Rebecca does not recognize the disguised *Ivanhoe,* but quite willingly tells this friendly stranger about her devotion to *Ivanhoe.* The dramatic complication depends on Rebecca's early promise to Cedric to refuse any proposals from his disobedient son; learning the couple have now rediscovered their love, he drives them out.

After the necessary dungeon scenes, castle interviews, and the histrionic spectacle of a near burning at the stake, *Ivanhoe* and Rebecca's affection has survived the severest tests, and marriage seems certain. In the best traditions of domestic melodrama, marriage (a kind of new birth) cannot occur without a death, one that frees the individual from an earlier attachment. When Isaac dies in the last scene (assumably the cultural shock of his daughter's impending marriage kills him), Rebecca can freely accept *Ivanhoe* as her husband.

Soane disagrees with Scott's view that "it is a dangerous and fatal doctrine to teach . . . that rectitude of conduct and of principle are . . . adequately rewarded by the gratification of our passions or attainment of our wishes" (545). Even though the novel's ending remains distinctly masculine, with the hero having regained his health in time to set things right, Scott shares a sympathy with contemporary women novelists who felt their characters, especially women, were controlled by events rather than masters of them. Soane's adaptation becomes in effect a rejection of what Jane Austen and Scott had learned about individual aspirations, rebuking self-centeredness and personal ambition. Soane denies the plight of the individual caught up in a mechanistic world and ignores the prevailing truth of women's serfdom.

All melodrama relies on musical elements, whether by introducing songs, using instrumental sequences to mark the acting, or creating an entire musical drama. *Ivanhoe; or the Knight Templar,* first performed at Covent Garden on 2 March 1820, serves as an important bridge between the early drama containing some musical numbers and the later complete operas. Samuel Beazley wrote the text and the music, often relying on the plain English ballad, much to the delight of his audience. Part of the pleasure came from his choice of singing parts for Robin Hood and his outlaws and for Rowena and *Ivanhoe*, but Beazley sensed the value of Scott's minor characters and enhanced their parts in the drama. The comic love duet of Elgitha and Wamba serves as a wonderful parallel to Rebecca and De Bracey's musical numbers, as she fends him off while awaiting her true lover's arrival.

Beazley altered Scott's narrative, increasing the comic opportunities and balancing these against tragic scenes. These experiments, as interesting as they are, really anticipate what the composer and librettist would do with the novel in the serious business of opera.

For nearly 400 years the opera has been one of the most alluring forms of musical entertainment. A special glamour attaches to everything connected with it—the vocal and instrumental music, soloists, ensembles, and orchestra, not to mention the drama, visual effects, and acting. The public for generations has been drawn to the work of our greatest writers whose characters, themes, and stories have been brought to life on the opera stage. Understandably, Shakespeare's plays have provided more riches for opera than any other source, yet as a close second Scott's novels stand as the inspiration for more operas than any other single writer. At least 50 operas are based on his works, and the results of turning a novel into an opera give one a new appreciation for Scott's genius.

The Scott operas are all products of the nineteenth century, and as it happened, time, place, and the personalities of novelist and composers were happily met. From Gioacchino Rossini's *La Donna del Lago* (1819) to several works of the 1890s—Reginald De Koven's *Rob Roy,* Isidore De Lara's *Amy Robsart,* J. Klein's *Kenilworth,* Hamish MacCunn's *Jeanie Deans,* Alick Maclean's *Quentin Durward,* and Arthur Sullivan's *Ivanhoe*—these operas rely on a variety of styles, from the feast of color, movement, and sound typical of romantic opera and opera-comique to the Wagner-influenced music dramas.

Ivanhoe has inspired nine operas (ten if one includes Beazley's 1820 musical drama); according to Jerome Mitchell, only the music and text for seven remain extant.[36] One of the earliest and the best known—partly because of Scott's presence in the audience and his intriguing *Journal* comment—was Rossini's *Ivanhoe.* For the 1826 season two Parisian librettists, Emile Deschamps and Gustave deWailly, decided on using music from four Rossini operas, *Semiramide, Mose, Tancredi,* and *LaGazza Ladra,* to create this popular pastiche. Scott enjoyed the performance with the Norman soldiers in pointed helmets and hauberks of mail and was undisturbed with whatever poetic license the librettists had taken with his story. He had no reaction to the ornate but lively music, commenting only on the strange sounds his words produced when "recited in a foreign tongue and for the amusement of a strange people."[37]

Deschamps, who was responsible in part for the introduction of Romanticism into French opera, wrote the *Ivanhoe* libretto with three concerns in mind. The novel provides far too much material for a successful operatic libretto, so minor characters (even major figures like Rowena and Robin Hood) are left out and memorable scenes are compressed into one. Fortunately, most Scott novels divide neatly into a few great scenes. By redirecting the emphasis and using selective omission, Deschamps skillfully consolidates the Rotherwood action and the Torquilstone siege into one act, with the final two acts set near or in the chateau de Saint-Edmond (the Templestowe of the novel). Since Scott relies on characters speaking directly to other figures or delivering soliloquies, the *Ivanhoe* librettists could convert these speeches into arias with little difficulty. By exploiting a single emotional strain in each aria, the librettist often pressed his meaning on the audience by using a motto phrase at the beginning, from which the ensuing ideas originated. If Scott sensed the "strangeness" of his language, it was more than likely because Deschamps had changed the diction and phraseology to suit his own purposes.

When a particular aspect seems especially compelling, Deschamps expands it, increasing the opportunity for musical possibilities. With a keen sense for the politically correct, he converts the Jews, Isaac and Rebecca, to the Moslems, Ismael and Leila, avoiding any hint of anti-Semitism. These two appear at Cedric's chateau, having left the lists of Ashby pursued by Bois-Guilbert's cutthroats. (In the novel, Isaac had come alone, and the Ashby tournament had not taken place.) The value of having Leila appear now in the story, especially since no other major female character exists, is to give the couple's relationship (*Ivanhoe* is present in the guise of the Pilgrim) early dramatic emphasis, as well as to introduce two emotionally climactic arias.

The arias were the crux of *Ivanhoe,* and Scott's flair for the dramatic gave the librettists' vocal consciousness real impetus. Now imprisoned at Saint-Edmond, Leila sends notes imploring *Ivanhoe* to rescue her, or at least inform the French King, whose army is in England marking the end of a truce between the two countries. Leila sings an aria declaring her total devotion: "love reigns in her soul and triumphs over duty. Her heart burns to see [*Ivanhoe*]; his very presence will relieve her suffering" (Mitchell, 151). Such a declaration has no parallel in the novel, and finally the most unexpected turn of events occurs.

Early in act 1 Cedric recalls his soldiering days in the Holy Land 15 years before, when his friend Olric, the last male descendant of the Saxon royal house, had been killed and Olric's daughter, Edith, captured. Now, at the end of the opera when *Ivanhoe* has gone to the rescue of Leila, it seems that Ismael, who apparently fears for his daughter's life, can no longer keep hidden the secret of her true identity. As it turns out, Leila is Edith; the daughter of the Saxon prince lives; Cedric, overjoyed at the prospects, can hardly wait until *Ivanhoe*'s victory is announced before telling him. *Ivanhoe* does the expected and proposes marriage to the eligible and Christian, Edith. The opera manages rather boldly in satisfying the desires of most readers for a more permanent liaison between Rebecca and *Ivanhoe*. Deschamps creates numerous opportunities for singing parts while tightening the pacing of Scott's novel. His desire for preserving the Italian bel canto style (the reason for choosing Rossini) over the French grand opera gave fuller flavor to the *Ivanhoe*-Rebecca relationship. Though important Scott characters are left out, Deschamps develops Rebecca as more passionate in temperament, and *Ivanhoe*'s sometimes pasteboard characteristics are enhanced with more forceful, intriguing qualities.

The other *Ivanhoe* operas continue the pattern of introducing Rebecca early and increasing the dramatic tension as Bois-Guilbert becomes a more creditable lover who suffers under the presence of an evil, supernatural force. In Heinrich Marschner's *Der Templer und die Judin* (1829), Rebecca's grandest moment is in the climactic trial scene, during which she calls out for a champion and Bois-Guilbert begs for the opportunity.[38] Faced with publicly declaring his support, he refuses and broods, lamenting the loss of his love. This German grand opera captures and improves on nearly all of the dramatic possibilities involving Rebecca and Bois-Guilbert.

A series of Italian composers found inspiration for *Ivanhoe* operas: Giovanni Pacini in *Ivanhoe* (1832), Otto Nicolai in *Il Templano* (1840), and Bartolomeo Pisani in *Rebecca* (1865). Each concentrates on the love interest between Rebecca and *Ivanhoe* and confronts the dilemma in rather ingenious ways. One librettist has Rowena as *Ivanhoe*'s sister, and she, though loving him, must relinquish him to Rebecca, who turns out to be Saxon too. Another approach finds *Ivanhoe* behaving in a heartlessly cold manner toward Rebecca, who, though devoted to him, cannot imagine openly revealing her affection. Pisani and librettist Piave created a surprising first act set in Palestine. Violating Scott's novelistic principle of self-control, the opera plunges immediately into the highly emotional material. Isaaco prepares to flee Palestine for England with Rebecca, since the open warfare of Christian and Saracen has endangered them. A Templar nearly assaults Rebecca, who escapes with the help of a young knight, Guilfredo. She returns the favor while caring expertly for his wounds. As the couple fall in love à la *Romeo and Juliet*, the parent wrenches his daughter away, leaving the suitor alone. All the melodramatic aspects combine with melody, vitality, and the exotic. Scott's color and grand spectacle seem well suited to Pisani's gifts.

The most stunning adaptation remains Arthur Sullivan's *Ivanhoe*, where nothing is omitted that would make the opera gripping, dramatic, and suspenseful. Sullivan, with his favorite partner, William S. Gilbert, was the genius of English comic opera. Early in his career, Sullivan, under Scott's influence, had composed a well-received cantata *Kenilworth* (1864) and an orchestral overture *Marmion* (1867), but his one serious work was reserved for *Ivanhoe*. Critics argued with Sullivan's complete devotion to comic opera as a squandering of his great talent. In part as an answer to these comments, he turned in the last decade of his life once again to Scott and the masterwork he hoped to create. Because of a recent argument and a general refusal to renounce the operetta, Gilbert left Sullivan, who collaborated instead with the librettist Julian Sturgis for his grand opera *Ivanhoe,* which opened at the Royal English Opera House in January 1891.

Unfortunately, this romantic opera was deemed an artistic and commercial failure, though it ran for more than 150 consecutive performances. Sullivan revised it for a new opera company in 1895 and was even inspired with further medievalism to project an opera on King Arthur. *Ivanhoe* appeared in Berlin and was revived by Thomas Beecham at Covent Garden in 1910. Great effort and money were expended on magnificent scenery, a double cast, 12 horses in full trappings, 25 Scots Guards, and a burning scene at Torquilstone castle. Even with such pomp and circumstance, reviewers found a lack of dramatic continuity and focus; as if Scott's content was captured, but not his spirit, subtlety, and humor. A generally negative response did close the 1910 show early, yet its fascination for Sullivan devotees and fans of romantic opera revived *Ivanhoe* in 1973 at Hurlington School Theater, London.[39]

Sullivan, who deeply admired Scott, finally realized his own eclectic style did not lend itself to the large-scale structure or the emotional depth of *Ivanhoe.* The broad canvas scenes had potential for the operatic stage, but not for Sullivan's miniaturist strengths. It was this pictorial element, in fact, which had made a profound impression on another group of artists, who cheerfully exploited the changing attitudes of their discipline toward narrative material.

From 1814 to 1870 over 300 painters displayed more than 1000 "Scott" works at the Royal Academy and other British exhibitions.[40] If one broadens the field of Scott mania, artists are found who created character replicas in pottery, illustrated books, travel guides, jeweled keepsakes, and 54 submissions for the design competition for the Scott monument in Edinburgh.

Why would visual artists, especially painters, find Scott's works a fertile, even irresistible, resource for ideas? His range of subject matter is astounding, with historical events and settings extending over eight centuries of European history. Changes in the popularity of various classes of pictures were also occurring as British portraitists gave way to more intimate pictures, abandoning the highly formal language of Joshua Reynolds and Thomas Gainsborough. Genre, or subject painting, overran its rival landscape painting with an increasing interest in literary and historical topics. This bias for the narrative in painting emerged as the novel established itself as the leading literary genre, commenting with self-assurance on nineteenth-century social, political, and cultural life.

Within two years of *Waverley,* a variety of narrative scenes, character portraits, and even animal scenes had been selected from the novel as appropriate topics for illustration. More paintings were to follow from Scott's other novels. The painting done for exhibition and sale was only the first stage; the same image, if a hit, could become a small engraving, selling thousands of impressions. Beginning in the 1830s popular annuals often relied on reproductions of new pictures; these miniatures were done so skillfully that the smallest mark of character could be retained. Soon after, book illustration began representing even the most elevating ideas in a familiar vocabulary. When Scott or Dickens had social engineering as a theme in a particular novel, Richard Westall or Thomas Stothard would dramatically illustrate the moral content, as in the plates for the editions of *Tales of My Landlord* (1820) and *Ivanhoe* (1821).

By 1830 nearly every one of Scott's major novels (1814–26) had become a source for narrative art. Catherine Gordon's exhaustive and reliable study, *British Painting of Subjects from the English Novel,* shows *Ivanhoe* "studies" represent more than 20 percent of all paintings drawn from Scott's works. A comparison of the differing treatments of *Ivanhoe* clearly reveals the painters' general approach: illustrate specific scenes as representative of virtue, vice, or moral equilibrium.

The most frequent subject in what can be called a series is Rebecca, who plays an iconic role in the novel synonymous with generosity, compassion, selflessness, and love. John Martin's *Rebecca and the Knight Templar* (1836) captures "the fair woman in desolation" on a high battlement, threatened by Bois-Guilbert, who looks for all the world like the reincarnation of Hans Holbein's *Henry VIII.* Martin relies on various emblems suggestive of Romantic melodrama, the disparity of scale between the figure and the fantastic landscape is the most obvious effect. His technique seems rather theatrical, with the colossal architecture of Templestowe dominating the two characters who are shown gesturing to each other in a stock manner.

Andrew Geddes, the Scottish portrait and subject painter, who had done a well-known and lovely portrait of Scott, painted in oils *The Jewess, Rebecca*, in 1841. Though unfairly accused of discovering a scheme for selling sad portraits of women by labelling them as literary characters, Geddes captures in *Rebecca* her sensitivity with all the delicacy Scott would have required. If virtue and the ineffable qualities of moral equanimity can be rendered in paint, he has done so, but without sacrificing the sensual and sentimental qualities that define Rebecca's final melancholic vision.

Painters and illustrators of *Ivanhoe* shifted their interest from character studies of Rebecca (with at least 32 canvases) to more vigorous, crowded scenes typical of historical paintings. Daniel Maclise's *Robin Hood* (1841) and Richard Westall's (1821) untitled book illustration for *Ivanhoe* reflect Scott's humanizing influence on historical figures; instead of the smoothness and vacuity of restored Greek sculpture, the outlaw and his men are rendered without inhibitions, thoroughly optimistic, and one with the great forest that forms the setting. Maclise portrays King Richard as seated, while Robin Hood, the benevolent warrior, stands nearby; both men raise their cups in mutual congratulations for the Torquilstone victory. This intimate moment relives the narrative scene; abstractions of greatness are replaced by a reality of men who regard nature as a source of health, calm, and moral law. History domesticated is what Scott intended, and Maclise has the artistic capacity to realize and advance these ambitions.

Four years later Maclise submitted *The Spirit of Chivalry* to a fresco competition for the Lords Chamber in the new Palace at Westminster (a commission he received in 1846). The artist had spent more than a decade immersing himself in the cult of revivalist chivalry and medievalism. Maclise's appreciation for Scott's ethical thesis, which serves as the core of *Ivanhoe*, informed his selection of representative chivalric qualities. The main figure, a tall woman dressed in Saxon robes who combines Rebecca's dark beauty and Rowena's nobility and confident air, represents chivalry. Flanked by her chief devotees, a knight, modeled on Maclise's earlier portrait of King

Richard, and a bishop, the Spirit of Chivalry in all her glory looks down upon the Knight Initiate. He has the virtues of the young *Ivanhoe* (or as we would imagine him before leaving England for the Holy Land): devotion, strength of purpose, clarity of vision, youthful enthusiasm, and physical purity. Once again Maclise would ignore the stains of historical reality (murders, adultery, other acts of moral violence) for an allegorical (chivalric) approach. In doing so he simplifies Scott's deeper vision, choosing early Victorian idealism instead of Romantic contradictions and uncertainties.

Artists, after 1860, began selecting other literary sources, though interest in Scott continued, with as many as 15 paintings a year created to the end of the century. What did not change, however, was *Ivanhoe*'s appeal to the vast numbers of common humanity who could identify with the novel's intrigue, revolution, and change. They understood, if not intellectually certainly instinctually, that a world had been lost and a new age of science and technology loomed ahead. The eventual message of Scott's work provides a nostalgic, wistful conjuring up of the past and yet an optimistic belief in humankind's ability to puzzle out the difficulties and paradoxes of the new order.

Student Responses to Ivanhoe

The following brief comments were written by students in my honors literature class at North Carolina Wesleyan College in the spring of 1991. The course was a lecture-discussion; students were encouraged to speak in class and to contribute written responses at the end of each hour. I collected these, read them, responded with my own comments, and returned them at the beginning of the next class. I have chosen a small representative sample: the efforts, often compelling, would have perhaps made Scott proud.

Rebecca empathizes so much with her fellow human beings that their suffering fills her with agony of such intensity that she can barely stand to watch the fighting at Torquilstone. She is, first and foremost, a healer, a person who has dedicated her life to the principle (often associated with Christian teaching) of aiding those who are in need. Violence is the antithesis of her nature; she is far too compassionate to accept the violence and suffering that are an integral part of chivalry.

—Douglas Lentz

Ivanhoe undergoes a series of trials that take his virtue to a higher plane. His first trials are the five jousts with the knights at Ashby. The quality of his virtue is made apparent when he answers the Templar's question regarding his death: "I am fitter to meet death than thou art" (96). This reply tells the reader that not only is Ivanhoe in superb physical condition, but he is also fit spiritually—much more so than the Templar. When the reader learns of Ivanhoe's injury, one's reaction is disappointment. And although his wound keeps him out of a good part of the novel, the fact that Ivanhoe could be injured is one of the greatest qualities Scott could have given him. In his capacity for suffering and fallibility, as in his early prejudice against the Jews, Ivanhoe, Scott proves to the reader, is indeed human. Eventually he overcomes many of his physical and moral weaknesses and becomes a more realistic hero.

—Austin Jackson

Scott does not allow Ivanhoe to marry Rebecca because he is a realistic writer, not a romantic one. Idealistically Ivanhoe and Rebecca should be married because they are both admirable characters and deserve to have a "happily ever after" ending. Scott, however, is a realist. In our lives we don't always get what we want. Neither do we always get what we deserve or what we have earned. Often there seems no explanation for the bad things that happen to good people. Many times in Scott's novel the reader's wishes or desires for good characters are not granted. Goodness often finds no reward; this is a part of our lives. Why then would it not be a part of our literature?

—Michelle Cahoon

Rebecca is like the herbs in my garden in that we know each herb has to be rubbed or crushed to smell the aroma and to be able to enjoy its full flavor. Rebecca's true love, beauty, sensitivity, and wisdom come to light as she meets with adversity; as she is crushed, her innermost attributes appear. The more Rebecca is trodden on, the more resilient she becomes, and all those around her are affected by her strength and goodness.

—Elizabeth Hobbs

Chivalry was used to justify killing by glorifying physical strength and ignoring its violence and bloodshed; therefore, entering into combat became a proof of one's masculinity. The Ashby tournament was held to create battle scenes in which the participants used real weapons and could rarely be victorious without severely injuring each other. So in essence the spectators and participants were really going to war, complete with the desire to kill each other. The spectators desired the sight of blood as much as the typical Rambo fan of today. Scott impresses upon us the true ignorance of the spectators by making us continually aware of their actions.

—Mark Peterson

At the end of the novel, Ivanhoe is reconciled with his father, and now is able to formally ask Rowena to marry him. But his character shares the qualities of his two "fathers": Cedric and Richard. Like Richard, Ivanhoe is a romantic. Rowena has always been his love and no one has ever swayed his heart from her—no one until Rebecca. Ivanhoe is similar to Cedric in that he is a firm believer in tradition. Especially now as the father and son have been reconciled, Ivanhoe will not tamper with cultural and familial traditions to marry a Jewess. Ivanhoe has rediscovered his identity, and the realist in him represses any remaining romantic notions.

—Carey Knupp

In chapter 24 Bois-Guilbert shows himself for the contemptible individual he really is, and we should be careful not to forget the threat he poses to civil order. His words—"think not we long remained blind to the idiotical folly of our founders . . . our order soon adopted bolder and wider views" (255)—suggest just how corrupt the Templars have become, and how his own arrogance has warped his sense of consideration for others.

—Angela Boone

Ivanhoe and Rebecca did not marry because, aside from their religious and cultural differences, their thought processes were not compatible.

Rebecca was too outspoken, especially for a woman. Ivanhoe felt threatened by her accusations and convictions toward chivalry. Although he admired Rebecca's ability to think, he preferred Rowena, who more willingly accepted her subordinate status in the male-dominated society. She did not question Ivanhoe's actions, but just accepted his explanation and reasoning for them. Rebecca, however, was much more defiant. Ivanhoe would have never married someone whom he could not control.

—Lory Stevens

The Norman government and military show a sophistication the Saxons could never equal in either strength or organization. King Richard is the ideal Norman ruler, having proved himself not only in battle as the Black Knight but also as a just and merciful king. His absence, however, permits the rise of the evil John. Cedric, the "king" of the Saxons, is a poor example of both ruler and knight. His only authority is in reigning over his household, and with the banishment of Ivanhoe he ensures Rotherwood's destruction. Though I admire his resentment and resistance of Norman corruption, he cannot serve as a model leader for a new nation.

—Robin Parker

Ivanhoe helps initiate the overthrow of Prince John and the reestablishment of Richard as ruler and, as a result, is looked upon as a hero. However, he really does not earn this honor. His inner character lacks the strength typical of the hero. In fact all his conflicts have been resolved through the actions of outside forces. At Ashby the Black Knight saves him; when he is wounded, Isaac and Rebecca nurse him. When he is trapped in the burning Torquilstone castle, again it is "the forces of light" who had to save him from the fire. And in the final battle between the Templar and Ivanhoe, it was an act of God or else the author's creativity that allows him merely to touch the Templar to kill him, rather than the force of the Templar's intended blow killing him. In all these instances Ivanhoe's weak moral character—his striving for glory and lack of personal remorse for injuring or killing someone—proves his inability to answer a higher spiritual calling. Chivalry is an obstacle to Christian piety.

—Judy Boyd

Notes

1. Avrom Fleishman, *The English Historical Novel: Walter Scott to Virginia Woolf* (Baltimore: Johns Hopkins University Press, 1971), 19.

2. "*Monthly Magazine,* February, 1820," in *Scott: The Critical Heritage,* ed. John O. Hayden (New York: Barnes and Noble, 1970), 177; hereafter cited in text as *CH*.

3. Sir Walter Scott, *Ivanhoe,* ed. A. N. Wilson (London: Penguin Books, 1986), 526–27. All subsequent references are to this edition.

4. E. M. Forster, *Aspects of the Novel* (1927; New York: Harcourt, Brace, 1954), 52.

5. Alice Chandler, "Chivalry and Romance: Scott's Medieval Novels," *Studies in Romanticism* 14 (1975): 185–200.

6. Jane Millgate, *Walter Scott: The Making of the Novelist* (Toronto: University Press of Toronto, 1984), ix; hereafter cited in text.

7. See also Giorgio Vasari, *Lives of the Artists: A Selection* (New York: Noonday Press, 1965), 276.

8. Judith Wilt, *Secret Leaves: The Novels of Walter Scott* (Chicago: University Press of Chicago, 1985), 19; hereafter cited in text.

9. Francis R. Hart, *Scott's Novels: The Plotting of Historical Survival* (Charlottesville: University Press of Virginia, 1966), 160; hereafter cited in text.

10. From Lady Louisa Stuart, 16 January 1820, in *The Letters of Sir Walter Scott,* ed. H. J. C. Grierson, 12 vols. (London: Constable, 1934), 6:115–16; hereafter cited in text as *Letters*.

11. Marilyn Butler, *Romantics, Rebels and Reactionaries: English Literature and Its Background, 1760–1830* (New York: Oxford University Press, 1982), 109–12. See Mark Twain, *Life on the Mississippi* (New York: Bantam Books, 1985), 315–17, in his chapter "Enchantments and Enchanters."

12. Wolfgang Iser, *The Implied Reader: Patterns of Communication in Prose Fiction from Bunyan to Beckett* (Baltimore: Johns Hopkins University Press, 1978), 81–100.

13. Thomas Chatterton (1752–70), an English poet, who wrote a series of fake poems purported to be the work of a medieval Bristol cleric, Thomas Rowley. The ruse was successful for a short time.

14. Sir Walter Scott, *Rob Roy,* ed. Edgar Johnson (Boston: Houghton Mifflin, 1956), 3.

15. Francis R. Hart, "Scott's Endings: The Fictions of Authority," *Nineteenth-Century Fiction* 33 (1978): 52; hereafter cited in text.

16. See Scott's influence on future novelists in Judith Wilt, "Steamboat Surfacing: Scott and the English Novelists," *Nineteenth-Century Fiction* 35 (1981): 459–86; hereafter cited in text.

17. Northrop Frye, *Anatomy of Criticism: Four Essays* (Princeton: Princeton University Press, 1957), 139–40.

18. See Alexander Welsh, *The Hero of the Waverley Novels* (New York: Atheneum, 1968), chapter 4 on property (93–126); hereafter cited in text.

19. Edgar Johnson, *Sir Walter Scott: The Great Unknown* (New York, Macmillan, 1970), 1:369; hereafter cited in text.

20. I am heavily indebted in this section to Edgar Rosenberg's *From Shylock to Svengali: Jewish Stereotypes in English Fiction.* (Stanford: Stanford University Press, 1960), 92–102.

21. Geoffrey Chaucer, "Pardoner's Tale," *The Complete Poetry and Prose of Geoffrey Chaucer,* ed. John H. Fisher (New York: Holt, 1977), 221–31.

22. Kenneth Sroka, "The Function of Form: *Ivanhoe* as Romance," *Studies in English Literature* 19 (1979): 652; hereafter cited in text.

23. Chris R. Vanden Bossch, "Culture and Economy in *Ivanhoe,*" *Nineteenth-Century Literature* 42 (1987): 46–72.

24. Kurt Wittig, *The Scottish Tradition in Literature* (Edinburgh: Oliver and Boyd, 1958), 236.

25. Eino Railo, *The Haunted Castle: A Study of the Elements of English Romanticism* (New York: Humanities Press, 1964), 145.

26. Francis Bacon, "Observations on a Libel," *Works,* ed. James Spedding *et. al* (London, 1857–74), 5:384.

27. Mark Girouard, *The Return to Camelot: Chivalry and the English Gentleman* (New Haven: Yale University Press, 1981), 234.

28. Walter Scott, "Essay on Chivalry," in *The Miscellaneous Prose Works of Sir Walter Scott, Bart* (Boston: Wells and Lily, 1829), 6:14.

29. Daniel Cottom, *The Civilized Imagination: A Study of Ann Radcliffe, Jane Austen, and Sir Walter Scott* (Cambridge: Cambridge University Press, 1985), 127ff; hereafter cited in text.

30. Edgar Johnson, "Scott and the Corners of Time," in *Scott Bicentenary Essays,* ed. Alan Bell (Edinburgh: Scottish Academic Press, 1973), 37.

31. My knowledge of nineteenth-century feminist issues is indebted to Elaine Showalter's *Sexual Anarchy: Gender and Culture at the Fin de Siècle* (New York: Viking, 1990).

32. See Gary Kelly, *English Fiction of the Romantic Period: 1789–1830* (London: Longman, 1989), 157–60, and Johnson, "Scott and the Corners of Time," 18ff.

33. A. N. Wilson, *The Laird of Abbotsford: A View of Sir Walter Scott* (Oxford: Oxford University Press, 1989), 147.

34. *The Arthurian Revival in Victorian Art* (New York: Garland Publishers, 1990), 9; hereafter cited in text.

35. The various discussions of Scott adaptations are drawn from Henry A. White, *Sir Walter Scott's Novels on the Stage* (New Haven: Yale University Press, 1927), 102; Allardyce Nicoll, *A History of English Drama 1660–1900* (Cambridge: Cambridge University Press, 1976), 4:91–96; and Richard Ford, *Dramatisations of Scott's Novels: A Catalogue,* Oxford Bibliographical Society Occasional Publications no. 12 (1979).

36. This discussion of opera relies on Jerome Mitchell's *The Walter Scott Operas* (Tuscaloosa: University of Alabama Press, 1977), especially chapter 9 on *Ivanhoe;* hereafter cited in text.

37. *The Journal of Sir Walter Scott,* ed. W. E. K. Anderson (Oxford: Oxford University Press, 1972), 31 October 1826, 226.

38. Heinrich Marschner's opera opened in Leipzig and was performed for 20 years all over Europe. It was seen in New York in 1872 and had revivals in Germany in 1912–13.

39. The most recent evidence of this opera's popularity is its appearance as a compact disc recording: Authur Sullivan, *Ivanhoe,* conducted by Drummond Cowan and performed by the Prince Consort Orchestra and Chorus, Pearl, CDS-9615, 1990.

40. Catherine M. Gordon, *British Paintings of Subjects from the English Novel: 1740–1870* (New York: Garland Publishers, 1988), 141. See also Richard D. Altick, *Paintings from Books: Art and Literature in Britain, 1760–1900* (Columbus: Ohio State University Press, 1985).

Bibliography

Primary Works

Letters and Journal

The Journal of Sir Walter Scott. Edited by W. E. K. Anderson. Oxford: Oxford University Press, 1972.

The Letters of Sir Walter Scott. Edited by H. J. C. Grierson. 12 vols. London: Constable, 1932–37.

Corson, James C. *Notes and Index to Sir Herbert Grierson's Edition of the Letters of Sir Walter Scott.* Oxford: Clarendon Press, 1979.

The Miscellaneous Works of Sir Walter Scott. Edited by John G. Lockart. 28 vols. Edinburgh: Cadell, 1834–36.

The Waverley Novels

Opus Magnum. 48 vols. Edinburgh: Robert Cadell, 1830–34. The text was the last prepared by Scott for this edition.

Centenary Edition. 25 vols. Edinburgh: A. and C. Black, 1870–71.

Dryburgh Edition. 25 vols. London: Adam and Charles Black, 1892–94. *Ivanhoe* is volume 9.

Secondary Sources

Criticism—Books

Altick, Richard D. *Paintings from Books: Art and Literature in Britain, 1760–1900.* Columbus: Ohio State University Press, 1985. An impressive review of the powerful connections between art and literature; contains a full statement on Scott's popularity among painters.

Beiderwell, Bruce. *Power and Punishment in Scott's Novels.* Athens: University of Georgia Press, 1992. See references to *Ivanhoe*'s legal "authority."

Butler, Marilyn. *Romantics, Rebels and Reactionaries: English Literature and Its Background, 1760–1830.* New York: Oxford University Press, 1982. A superb analysis of Romantic literature set against its historical background.

Cottom, Daniel. *The Civilized Imagination: A Study of Ann Radcliffe, Jane Austen, and Sir Walter Scott.* Cambridge: Cambridge University Press, 1985. A sophisticated analysis of the conflicts between aristocratic and middle-class values in these writers' novels.

deGategno, Paul. *James Macpherson.* Boston: Twayne Publishers, 1989. Discusses Scott's early interest in Scottish antiquities and the function of the hero, including his role in the Ossianic controversy.

Dekker, George. *The American Historical Romance.* Cambridge: Cambridge University Press, 1987. Studies the Waverley novel as a new species of fiction that is concerned not only with eighteenth-century Scotland but also with a class of conflicts in the recent history of many countries.

Ferris, Ina. *The Achievement of Literary Authority: Gender, History, and the Waverley Novels.* Ithaca, N.Y.: Cornell University Press, 1991. See for references to *Ivanhoe*'s "canonical moment."

Frye, Northrop. *The Secular Scripture: A Study of the Structure of Romance.* Cambridge: Harvard University Press, 1976. Examines the characteristics of romance fiction in the Waverley Novels—a stimulating analysis.

Girouard, Mark. *The Return to Camelot: Chivalry and the English Gentleman.* New Haven: Yale University Press, 1981. Excellent discussion of the revival and adaptation of the medieval chivalric code in Britain from the eighteenth to the early twentieth centuries. Two chapters on Scott.

Hart, Francis R. *The Scottish Novel: From Smollett to Spark.* Cambridge: Harvard University Press, 1978. An expert's analysis of the two centuries of the Scottish novel. Highly dependable.

Kelly, Gary. *English Fiction of the Romantic Period: 1789–1830.* London: Longman, 1989. Contains an excellent chapter on Scott, with cogent comments in "The Romance of History: Ivanhoe to Redgauntlet."

Lauber, John. *Sir Walter Scott: Revised Edition.* Boston: Twayne Publishers, 1989. This edition integrates new scholarship. Treats Scott as a serious writer on the ideological issues of his time.

McMaster, Graham. *Scott and Society.* Cambridge: Cambridge University Press, 1982. This book provides a study of Scott's politics and his relation to the major intellectual currents of the age. Proposes the view that Scott's politics had more sanity and centrality than they have usually been given credit for.

Mennell, Stephen. *All Manners of Food: Eating and Taste in England and France from the Middle Ages to the Present.* Oxford: Basil Blackwell, 1986. Highly informative study on medieval gastronomy, or why the Normans ate what they did.

Millgate, Jane. *Walter Scott: The Making of the Novelist.* Toronto: University of Toronto Press, 1984. Studies Scott's authorial persona and the conventions of the new fictional subgenre he was creating.

Mitchell, Jerome. *Scott, Chaucer, and Medieval Romance: A Study in Sir Walter Scott's Indebtedness to the Literature of the Middle Ages.* Lexington: University Press of Kentucky, 1987. Useful appraisal of Scott's knowledge of medieval literature.

Rosenberg, Edgar. *From Shylock to Svengali: Jewish Stereotypes in English Fiction.* Stanford: Stanford University Press, 1960. The best study of Jewish characters in Scott.

Shaw, Harry E. *The Forms of Historical Fiction: Sir Walter Scott and His Successors.* Ithaca, N.Y.: Cornell University Press, 1983. Suggests that Scott's historical vision was two-fold: rhetorical and evaluative. Maintains that many of the characteristics of *Ivanhoe,* such as a certain schizophrenia in Ivanhoe himself, results from placing a "modern hero" in the Middle Ages.

Tulloch, Graham. *The Language of Walter Scott.* London: Andre Deutsch, 1980. Finds that the dialogue of *Ivanhoe* is not Anglo-Saxon or early Middle English but a mixed, artificially created language—a base of early nineteenth-century English with elements of earlier English added to give a flavor of antiquity.

Welsh, Alexander. *The Hero of the Waverley Novels, with New Essays on Scott.* 1968; Princeton: Princeton University Press, 1992. Valuable discussion of the hero motif.

Wilt, Judith. *Secret Leaves: The Novels of Walter Scott.* Chicago: University of Chicago Press, 1985. A critical study that is finely sensitive to Scott's language, especially the shared "Coming Home" theme in *Waverley* and *Ivanhoe.*

Criticism—Articles

Dawson, Terence. "Victims of Their Own Contending Passions: Unexpected Death in *Adolphe, Ivanhoe,* and *Wuthering Heights.*" *New Comparison,* 6 (1988): 83–100. Argues that the way characters die may be seen as a literary theme; sees Bois-Guilbert's death as crucial to the novel's resolution.

deGategno, Paul. "*Ivanhoe:* Novel, 1819." In *Beacham's Guide to Literature,* edited by S. Niemeyer. Washington, D.C.: Beacham Publishers, 1990: 1–7.

Eller, Ruth. "The Poetic Theme in Scott's Novels." In *Scott and His Influence,* edited by J. H. Alexander. Aberdeen, Scotland: Association for Scottish Literary Studies, 1983.

Giddings, Robert. "Scott and Opera." In *Sir Walter Scott: The Long-Forgotten Melody,* edited and introduced by Alan Bold. London: Vision, 1983. On operatic adaptation, especially the Arthur Sullivan and Julian Sturgis *Ivanhoe.*

Gifford, Douglas. "Scott's Fiction and the Search for Mythic Regeneration." In *Scott and His Influence,* edited by J. H. Alexander. Aberdeen, Scotland: Association for Scottish Literary Studies, 1983.

Hart, Francis R. "Scott's Endings: The Fictions of Authority." *Nineteenth-Century Fiction* 33 (1978): 48–68. Proposes that Scott's narratives, viewed as "fictions of restored authority," establish closure despite the paradox of placing authority in the past.

Johnson, Edgar. "Scott and the Corners of Time." In *Scott Bicentenary Essays,* edited by Alan Bell. Edinburgh: Scottish Academic Press, 1973.

Ragussis, Michael. "Writing Nationalist History: England, the Conversion of the Jews, and *Ivanhoe.*" *English Literary History* 60 (1993): 181–215. Argues for locating *Ivanhoe* at the international crossroads of one of the more important nineteenth-century political questions: the relation between national identity and alien populations.

Reizov, Boris G. "History and Fiction in Walter Scott's Novels." *Neohelicon* 1–2 (1974): 166–75. Discusses in general Scott's ability to give equal standing to truth and fiction in his novels. Specifically argues this point as it relates to *Ivanhoe.*

Salari, Marinella. "Ivanhoe's Middle Ages." In *Medieval and Pseudo-Medieval Literature,* edited by Piero Boitani and Anna Torti. Cambridge, England: D. S. Brewer, 1984. Discusses *Ivanhoe* by focusing on the following themes: Ulysses, inheritance/disinheritance, disguise, the importance of clothes and food, and Scott's relation to the medieval period.

Scott, P. H. "The Politics of Sir Walter Scott." In *Scott and His Influence,* edited by J. H. Alexander. Aberdeen, Scotland: Association for Scottish Literary Studies, 1983.

Shaw, Harry E. "Scott and George Eliot: The Lure of the Symbolic." In *Scott and His Influence,* edited by J. H. Alexander. Aberdeen, Scotland: Association for Scottish Literary Studies, 1983.

Simeone, William E. "The Robin Hood of *Ivanhoe.*" *Journal of American Folklore* 74 (1961): 230–34. Maintains that Scott gives Robin Hood a moral perfection that is consistent with the Romantic idea of the natural nobility of the common man.

Sutherland, Kathryn. "Fictional Economics: Adam Smith, Walter Scott, and the Nineteenth-Century Novel." *English Literary History* 54 (Spring 1987): 97–127. Maintains that in writing novels Scott reached an accommodation between the way he understood "the nature and status of authorship" and his participation in a new commercial and social science.

Thurber, Barton. "Scott and the Sublime." In *Scott and His Influence,* edited by J. H. Alexander. Aberdeen, Scotland: Association for Scottish Literary Studies, 1983.

Vanden Bossche, Chris. "Culture and Economy in *Ivanhoe.*" *Nineteenth-Century Literature* 42 (1987): 46–72. Suggests the novel dramatizes culture as a semiotic system that constitutes social relations; the theme of language is a metaphor for culture.

Biographies

Grierson, H. *Sir Walter Scott, Bart.* 1938; New York: Haskell, 1969. Good one-volume biography written by the editor of Scott's letters.

Johnson, Edgar. *Sir Walter Scott: The Great Unknown.* 2 vols. New York: Macmillan, 1970. The current standard biography.

Wilson, A. N. *The Laird of Abbotsford: A View of Sir Walter Scott.* Oxford: Oxford University Press, 1989. Subtle and enthusiastic critical biography; contains a number of specific references to *Ivanhoe* and a chapter devoted to "Scott's Medievalism."

Bibliographies

Corson, James C. *A Bibliography of Sir Walter Scott . . . 1797–1940.* 1943; New York: B. Franklin, 1969.

Rubenstein, Jill. *Sir Walter Scott: A Reference Guide.* Boston: G. K. Hall, 1978. Writings about Scott from 1932–1977.

Index

The Author

Paul J. deGategno, 1992–93 Jefferson-Pilot Professor of English and chair of the Division of Humanities at North Carolina Wesleyan College, was educated at Norwich University in Vermont, the University of Rhode Island, and The Pennsylvania State University. A former National Endowment for the Humanities fellow and Lilly scholar, he has published articles on Rochester, Defoe, Smollett, Radcliffe, Jefferson, and Scottish literature, and the book *James Macpherson* (1989), a study of the eighteenth-century Scottish poet and historian.